TRY THIS

RESEARCH METHODS FOR WRITERS

Practices & Possibilities

Series Editors: Aimee McClure, Mike Palmquist, and Aleashia Walton

Series Associate Editors: Lauryn Bolz and Jagadish Paudel

The Practices & Possibilities Series addresses the full range of practices within the field of Writing Studies, including teaching, learning, research, and theory. From Joseph Williams' reflections on problems to Richard E. Young's taxonomy of "small genres" to Adam Mackie's considerations of technology, the books in this series explore issues and ideas of interest to writers, teachers, researchers, and theorists who share an interest in improving existing practices and exploring new possibilities. The series includes both original and republished books. Works in the series are organized topically.

The WAC Clearinghouse and University Press of Colorado are collaborating so that these books will be widely available through free digital distribution and low-cost print editions. The publishers and the series editors are committed to the principle that knowledge should freely circulate and have embraced the use of technology to support open access to scholarly work.

Recent Books in the Series

Jessie Borgman and Casey McArdle (Eds.), *Pars in Practice: More Resources and Strategies for Online Writing Instructors* (2021)

Mary Ann Dellinger and D. Alexis Hart (Eds.), *ePortfolios@edu: What We Know, What We Don't Know, And Everything In-Between* (2020)

Jo-Anne Kerr and Ann N. Amicucci (Eds.), *Stories from First-Year Composition: Pedagogies that Foster Student Agency and Writing Identity* (2020)

Patricia Freitag Ericsson, *Sexual Harassment and Cultural Change in Writing Studies* (2020)

Ryan J. Dippre, *Talk, Tools, and Texts: A Logic-in-Use for Studying Lifespan Literate Action Development* (2019)

Jessie Borgman and Casey McArdle, *Personal, Accessible, Responsive, Strategic: Resources and Strategies for Online Writing Instructors* (2019)

Cheryl Geisler and Jason Swarts, Coding *Streams of Language: Techniques for the Systematic Coding of Text, Talk, and Other Verbal Data* (2019)

Ellen C. Carillo, *A Guide to Mindful Reading* (2017)

TRY THIS

RESEARCH METHODS FOR WRITERS

Jennifer Clary-Lemon

University of Waterloo

Derek Mueller

Virginia Tech

Kate Pantelides

Middle Tennessee State University

WAC Clearinghouse
wac.colostate.edu
Fort Collins, Colorado

University Press of Colorado
upcolorado.com
Louisville, Colorado

The WAC Clearinghouse, Fort Collins, Colorado 80523

University Press of Colorado, Louisville, Colorado 80027

ISBN 978-1-64215-144-2 (PDF) | 978-1-64215-145-9 (ePub) | 978-1-64642-312-5 (pbk.)

DOI 10.37514/PRA-B.2022.1442

Produced in the United States of America

Library of Congress Cataloging-in-Publication Data

Names: Clary-Lemon, Jennifer, author. | Mueller, Derek N., 1974– author. | Pantelides, Kate, 1981– author.
Title: Try this : research methods for writers / Jennifer Clary-Lemon, University of Waterloo ; Derek Mueller, Virginia Tech ; Kate Pantelides, Middle Tennessee State University.
Description: Fort Collins, Colorado : The WAC Clearinghouse ; Louisville, Colorado : University Press of Colorado, [2022] | Series: Practices & possibilities | Includes bibliographical references.
Identifiers: LCCN 2021060203 (print) | LCCN 2021060204 (ebook) | ISBN 9781646423125 (paperback) | ISBN 9781642151442 (pdf) | ISBN 9781642151459 (epub)
Subjects: LCSH: English language—Rhetoric—Research—Methodology. | English language—Rhetoric—Problems, exercises, etc. | Academic writing.
Classification: LCC PE1408 .C5227 2022 (print) | LCC PE1408 (ebook) | DDC 808/.042—dc23/eng/20220113
LC record available at https://lccn.loc.gov/2021060203
LC ebook record available at https://lccn.loc.gov/2021060204

Copyeditor: Karen Peirce
Designer: Mike Palmquist
Cover Art: Derek Mueller
Series Editors: Aimee McClure, Mike Palmquist, and Aleashia Walton
Series Associate Editors: Lauryn Bolz and Jagadish Paudel

The WAC Clearinghouse supports teachers of writing across the disciplines. Hosted by Colorado State University, it brings together scholarly journals and book series as well as resources for teachers who use writing in their courses. This book is available in digital formats for free download at wac.colostate.edu.

Founded in 1965, the University Press of Colorado is a nonprofit cooperative publishing enterprise supported, in part, by Adams State University, Colorado State University, Fort Lewis College, Metropolitan State University of Denver, University of Alaska Fairbanks, University of Colorado, University of Denver, University of Northern Colorado, University of Wyoming, Utah State University, and Western Colorado University. For more information, visit upcolorado.com.

Contents

Preface

Writing is often heralded as one of the most—if not the most—important skills one can hone in higher education. But we—three teacher-scholars in Writing Studies—argue that it's not just writing that matters. Composition is about thinking alongside others, about problem-solving, about experimentation, about the excitement, curiosity, and unsureness that comes with seeking questions to which we don't know the answer. Composing asks us to approach problems that are confusing, use tools we haven't before, invent genres for new rhetorical needs, and make texts using textual, audio, visual, and digital tools. Composition is about knowledge-making, not just writing about knowledge. This text invites students and faculty to approach composing at all levels with an openness and a willingness to be wrong and/or to discover something new and exciting.

There seems to be much agreement that writing also means researching. Whenever we compose, we draw on both what we know and what we don't know to seek answers. Yet, sometimes we get stuck in a rut, circling around the known, only using secondary textual research to answer our questions. In fact, "the research paper" is a stalwart of most writing classes, but we suggest that often, research papers don't invite students and faculty to the exciting work of not knowing, coming across new information, accessing primary data, and selecting research methods beyond secondary-source research. Research projects should be primarily exploratory, sometimes conclusive, but more often than not an opening-up of new unknowns, new spaces, and new questions. Of course, we have to share findings at some point, but research is almost always in progress, incomplete. In this text we offer multiple interdisciplinary methods—often used in research in the field, but rarely drawn upon in undergraduate courses—and suggest them for use at all levels. Such an approach to composition has energized our own research and teaching.

In *Try This: Research Methods for Writers*, we ask students and faculty to approach writing and researching differently than before. We invite you to revel with us in the unknown, in liminality, in the excitement of primary research. This shifts the approach from a standard model of knowledge delivery to a pedagogy of knowledge-making, from a standard model of research writing as solitary to an acknowledgement of research writing as collective, overlapping, and distributed. We offer methods for working with words, with people, with artifacts, with places, and with visuals. We start out with what we expect is more familiar in English Studies—rhetorical analysis, secondary source use, surveys, and interviews—and we move to methods that we think might be less familiar, though just as useful and engaging—discourse analysis, map-making, and using worknets for invention. Of course, you can work through the book in whatever way matches your writing and research needs, but we do encourage you to spend some time reading, thinking, and talking about the nature of research (Chapter 1) and how to develop ethical research (Chapter 2) as you begin your work together.

Each chapter is organized around methods to approach a particular kind of primary data—texts, artifacts, places, and images. Because reading about writing and research is never enough, there are "Try This" invention projects peppered throughout each chapter—these projects are designed to invite readers to "try" the ideas we have introduced. Some of these projects are designed to try during class time and take 5–15 minutes. Some require time and space and will take hours to accomplish. Some are extensive and will take days to accomplish. Each research writing opportunity introduced in a "Try This" invention project is designed to scaffold a research project. In addition to introducing different methods and "Try This" research writing opportunities, chapters also offer different culminating genres that allow research to circulate and to connect meaningfully with audiences. For instance, in addition to textual genres, we address scaffolding for digital research posters, data visualizations, and short-form presentations.

Try This emphasizes the centrality of curiosity and discovery, invention, and process to researching writers. We know that along the way, students and instructors may find this a messy process! It is our hope that in engaging with the richness that all research offers—whether working closely with texts, talking with people, observing locations, generating and analyzing visuals, and producing written texts—you will use this book as a guide through the most challenging and rewarding moments of your research practices.

TRY THIS
RESEARCH METHODS FOR WRITERS

Chapter 1. What are Research Methods?

Like all research projects, this text begins with questions: What is research? Who does research? Why do research?

Research is the systematic asking of questions and congruent use of methods to learn answers to interesting, important questions. Whether or not your research has been purposeful in the past, *you* do research all the time.

When you try to decide which deodorant is most effective by trying different brands, you're doing research. When you ask friends for recommendations about where to go to dinner, you're doing research. When you experiment with different routes to find the best way to get to work, you're doing research. And why? Because you want to know. Because you want to try to know. But such information-gathering often takes particular routes, requires specific tools, and is measured very differently. That's where research methods come in. If you buy deodorant, you test it on yourself, a human subject. If you ask friends for dinner reservations, you might send a group text that acts as a survey, see who weighs in, and find out if their opinions match. When you drive a particular route, you are engaging with a particular site and measuring time. Each of these ways of using particular tools to answer a question you have are different kinds of research methods.

Research methods are the tools, instruments, practices, processes—insert whatever making metaphor you prefer—that allow you to answer questions of interest and contribute to a **critical conversation**, or a grouping of recognized ideas about that interest. The critical conversation comes out of our preliminary discovery about a particular question or set of questions—discovery work known as **rhetorical invention**, or a starting place for thinking, researching, and writing. Just as an entrepreneur might invent an as-seen-on-TV product that comes out of months of consumer observations and materials testing, writers invent their ideas through gathering data in particular and diverse ways. That gathering place is the locus of research methods, which we separate out in this book as working with sources

(Chapter 3), working with words (Chapter 4), working with people (Chapter 5), working with places and things (Chapter 6), and working with visuals (Chapter 7). Here, it's important to note that the word "methods" is derived from the Greek terms *meta-* (above, beyond) and *-hodos* (routes, pathways).

Try This: Preview Your Awareness of Research Methods (15 minutes)

Think about the ways you've used different methods to solve problems and answer questions in your life, then begin to apply those experiences to your understanding of research methods:

1. Make brief lists of ways/tools/methods you know of (or make up a method—be creative!) to

   a. **work with sources** (the focus of Chapter 3 in this book). As a starting point, you might include different library databases you have accessed, or you might note various libraries you have visited—what else?

   b. **work with words or texts** (the focus of Chapter 4 in this book). As a starting point, you might include different patterns you might look for in a text, like how many times a word appears or how many times it appears in combination with a related word—what else?

   c. **work with people** (the focus of Chapter 5 in this book). As a starting point, you might consider that talking with folks individually is just one of the many ways of learning about them. What are some other ways to learn about people, their behaviors, and their opinions?

   d. **work with places and things** (the focus of Chapter 6). As a starting point, consider how the resources you can access at your university and the spaces you inhabit in your daily life impact your experience at the university. How might you systematically catalogue such observations?

   e. **work with visuals** (the focus of Chapter 7 in this book). As a starting point, you might just consider the visuals you have come across in the day so far. What were they? What did they communicate? How did they impact you? How can visuals share information about research, and how might they be the subject of a research project?

2. Test your invention work by turning to each chapter and scanning the methods we survey. Note, in particular, where we have given name to a method you identified but did not have a term for, where we have overlaps, where you identified an idea that we have not listed. The methods we consider in this text are just a starting point, and you may find that you need to combine them to get answers you're interested in, you may need to look for methods outside the text, or you may need to design a new method to accommodate your project.

Considered with this in mind, research methods train researchers on the available routes and pathways to generating new knowledge. Through writing and delivery (circulation), researchers and the texts they produce both participate meaningfully in and also continue to shape research conversations (i.e., what is known and what is knowable). Our approach in this text recognizes that you may have research questions about different areas of interest, so it is important to have access to multiple methods that might effectively lead you to a satisfying answer to your research question.

The thinking and decisions about research that we will ask you to make in this text are complex. Often textbooks are intended to boil down ideas to their simplest parts, but we are purposeful in offering complexity, both because we know students are smart and can make sense of it, and because interesting research is complex. You won't initially end up with clean, clear, easy answers, but that is by design. Real research is messy and requires rethinking. It often also includes periods of not-knowing, which can be uncomfortable. Get ready to take risks, to experiment, and to not find the answer on the first try.

The process the preceding "Try This" asks you to recall—that of identifying interesting questions, matching appropriate methods, considering possible answers, and reflecting on this process to improve it in future iterations—is the process of conducting research. In this text, we will encourage you to tap into this curiosity, innovation, and reflection and deploy it systematically in your academic research writing projects. As students you have the opportunity to contribute to our understanding of the world through your research. Instead of simply asking you to read what others have learned through research (which is also very important!), in this text we ask you to jump in right away and participate in knowledge-making. We will alternate between **invention**—opportunities for you to try out informal writing and activities related to your research question—and **delivery***—opportunities for you to develop specific writing products that get you closer to answering your research question. We will also ask you to compose in multiple genres (proposals, memos, literature reviews, maps, etc.) and modes (visual, written, oral, aural), a recognition that research takes many forms and relies on multiple senses.

We often spend a lot of time on delivery—the product of our reading, writing, and researching—but in this text we ask you to rebalance that attention to invention—starting points for reading, writing, and researching processes.

■ Uncertainty and Curiosity

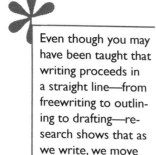

Even though you may have been taught that writing proceeds in a straight line—from freewriting to outlining to drafting—research shows that as we write, we move between and among these phases. Writing—and research—is far more like a tornado than a straight line.

Research does not start with a thesis statement. It starts with a question. And though research is **recursive,*** which means that you will move back and forth between various stages in your research and writing process, developing an effective question might in itself be the most important part of the research process. Because there's really no point in doing a research project if you already know the answer. That is boring. But it is how we are often taught to do research: we decide what we're going to argue, we look for those things that support that argument, and then we write up the thing that we knew from the outset. If that sounds familiar, we suggest that you scrap that plan.

Instead, we suggest approaching research with an orientation of openness, ready and willing to be surprised, to change your mind. Of course, you never approach research in a vacuum. You probably have ideas about whatever it is that you're working on. You probably have thoughts about what the answers are to your research questions, and that is as it should be, but that statement of belief should not be where you start.

Try This: Consider Everyday Contexts You Have Engaged in Research (15 minutes)

Take a moment to think about the many occasions when you have gathered information to answer a question outside of an academic context (i.e., What is the most effective deodorant? Where is the best place to eat? What is the fastest route home?):

1. First, make a list of some of these everyday questions you have identified and the answers you have come up with in your research.

2. Select one that is still interesting to you—one that you may have answered but suspect there are more answers to or one that the answer you identified was only partial.

3. Note the method or tool you selected to answer the question.

4. Make a list of other methods you might employ to answer your original question.

5. Reflect on how identifying alternative research methods might lead you to different answers to your original question, then make a new research plan.

We hope you cultivate an exploratory motive, an orientation of openness, and a willingness to learn. Adopting such a disposition is your work. Get ready to find data that conflicts with what you have come to know about a particular issue. You might even think about your thesis statement as the last thing that you develop in your research project. *Let curiosity drive you forward in your work.* Research is really only worth engaging in if you learn something from it.

We often think about research as knowing, but it's really about the *making* of knowledge(s), the movement from not knowing to beginning to know, figuring things out, trying to solve or sort out tricky problems. At the end of an effective research project, we usually have more questions than we started with. Sure, we answer the initial question (if all goes well), but that process of building knowledge usually leads to more questions and helps us recognize what we don't know.

Developing a research orientation includes seeing the world around you as abundant with research opportunities. Harness your curiosity, embrace uncertainty, and begin looking for researchable questions.

Try This: Make a List of Curios (30 minutes)

Reflect on times that you've gotten wrapped up in something—when you looked away from the clock and suddenly two hours had passed. What were you doing? Cooking, reading, engaging in a good conversation, playing a game, watching tv, hiking? Identify that experience and consider the following questions:

- What was it that made time fly?
- How might you capture that energy in a research experience?

Now make a curio cabinet of sorts. A curio is a special, mysterious object that inspires curiosity. Cabinets of curiosities were popularized in Europe in the late sixteenth century. They featured items from abroad and unique artifacts from the natural world. Such spaces allowed collectors to assemble and display collections that catalogued their interests and travels and that inspired awe in their reception. Create a curio cabinet for yourself, either by assembling a collection of artifacts that describe your interests, composing an image that represents your curiosities, or developing a textual representation of questions that interest you.

No matter where your research and writing take you—in terms of major, interest, or profession—it's useful to consistently reflect on what, why, and how you're conducting research at each step in the process. This attention to thinking about your thinking is called **metacognition**. This process may sound exhausting, and it can be, especially at first, but being metacognitive about your research will help you **transfer** your learning into new contexts. Having this orientation toward your research ensures that you have **intention** in each step you take. The more you practice this approach to research, the easier it gets so that it eventually becomes instinctual.

■ Rhetorical Foundations of Research

What we have described thus far is a **rhetorical approach** to the research process. Derived from classical Greek influences, the five ancient **canons** of rhetoric include **invention, arrangement, style, memory**, and **delivery**. In the context of writing and research, these long established, foundational concepts also go by other names, such as pre-writing, organization, mechanics and grammar, process, and circulation of a research product. We want to keep in mind these qualities of effective communication throughout the chapter, but we'll spend significant time with invention and delivery—canons that we think often get pushed aside or treated as afterthoughts in many approaches to research and research-based writing and that we pay particular attention to in this text.

As you familiarize yourself with an issue and the way scholars have talked about it, take note of the specific ways they talk about the issue and consider why that is. This is how you develop a rhetorical awareness of the ways in which research is constructed. So when you read, read like a researcher: consider both *what* is said about an issue and *how* it is said. Identify the **rhetorical situation** of the piece of writing; this includes the **context** in which it is written, the **audience** for whom it is written, and its **purpose**.

In this book, we aim to familiarize you with a range of research genres. We begin here with a research proposal, but throughout this book we also highlight other research genres that may be more or less familiar to you: literature reviews, coding schemas, annotated maps, research memos, slide decks, and posters. Each time you encounter a new genre, we encourage you to place it in its communicative context: What is the reason to compose this way? What need does it fulfill for its audience? What situation is it most suited to? What communication problem does it solve? We hope that working through research genres in this way will also help you understand your own research process more fully.

Try This: Go on a Scavenger Hunt to Identify Genres in "The Wild" (30 minutes)

With a partner or two, walk around identifying, photographing, documenting, and analyzing genres in your midst. If you're at a university, you might see posters, signs, and bulletin boards. If you're at home, you'll see different genres, and if you're at a coffee shop, you'll see yet another set of genres.

Consider this: one genre found in a coffee shop is a menu. It might be on a board, or there may be paper menus that each customer can pick up, but this genre is reliably found in coffee shops throughout the US. Wherever you are, be attentive to the genres that surround you by doing the following:

1. Make a list of the genres (the kind of texts) that make up your immediate environment.

2. Choose one genre that interests you and consider its rhetorical situation:

    a. What is the context in which it is written?

    b. Who is its audience?

    c. What is the genre's purpose?

3. More broadly, consider the genre's communicative context:

    a. How is this particular example of the genre composed?

    b. What communication problem does it solve?

How might such rhetorical knowledge about genre impact your approach to matching research questions to methods and delivery?

Research Example: Student Writing Habits

Let's use an example to illustrate what happens at the beginning of a research project. Like us, you might be interested in student writing habits. In particular, you might research *when* (and why) students begin a research project: Do they begin when it is assigned? Two weeks in advance? The night before?

Other researchers have looked at this issue, so you might begin by examining what they have found. These **secondary sources**, the findings of other thinkers, constitute the critical conversation and might give you ideas for how you might proceed in your own project (for a method to use for tracing sources and their connections, see Chapter 3). Thus, examining this conversation might function as **pre-writing**, **brainstorming**, or **invention** for your research. Rhetorician Kenneth Burke uses the metaphor of a party to describe how critical conversations work: When you arrive at the party, the conversations have been going on for a while, and guests take turns articulating their points of view, sometimes talking over each other, sometimes interrupting, laughing, disagreeing, and agreeing. After listening for a while, you understand the conversation and have something to say, so you chime in, maybe building on what a previous guest has said or contrasting your ideas with a friend's. Finally, you're tired and have to head home, but when you do, the sounds of the party are still ringing in your ears, and the conversation will clearly continue.

But if you're conducting **primary research** that moves beyond **working with sources**, the key is to next find out what this particular issue looks like in your local context, or in a specific context in which you're interested. Most likely, scholars have not examined the issue of when students begin their assignments at your institution, and many factors may impact your context that might make your findings different than what you've learned from other scholars. Research methods give researchers recognizable ways to continue the party conversation started by secondary sources.

So the next step is effective **research design**. You might articulate this plan in a **research proposal**, further detailed at the end of this chapter. When you are beginning a new research project, the design is expected to be mixed up and messy, because oftentimes you are sorting through many different possibilities. Thus, we encourage you to notice and to write about the messiness of an emerging research design, pausing often to pose the following questions: What are you wondering about *now*?* and, How are these curiosities connecting, drawing your attention to matters you hadn't considered before? While it's important to notice these inklings as you go, many effective researchers also write about them as a way to record (to help with memory) and focus. The activity of writing while researching demands patience and persistence, and yet the emerging research design will be magnitudes more refined in later stages as a result.

> Writing is a thinking process, not just a communication process. Integrate writing into your research process as a method for thinking through your ideas.

Design your research project so that your questions, methods, data, findings, and conclusions match up and so that you select or develop **primary source data** that will be most useful for your particular interest. For instance, if you only have data for about 30 students on campus, you can't generalize about how *all students* approach the writing process. If you only know when these students start working on a given writing project, you won't know why they started at that particular time. This doesn't mean the information you have isn't useful; it just means that you need to stay close to your data and only make sense of the information you have. Make note of things you want to know and wish you had more data about so you can develop the project if the opportunity arises.

For this research project on timing in student writing projects, you might develop a survey that asks students when they begin their research project as well as a series of related questions about motivation and timing. If you design a survey that gives students choices to select answers that range from "I begin a project when it is assigned" to "I begin a project the morning that it's due," you will develop **quantitative** data, or representative numbers, that answer your question. If you're interested in longer, more nuanced answers, you might also provide open-ended questions on your survey, and you'll develop both quantitative and **qualitative** data, or non-numeric data not organized according to a specific, numerical pattern.

A **survey** develops data that might be easily counted and categorized and can be offered to many folks. But you might be interested in more specific, extensive qualitative data than what you can gather through a survey. Your interest might be not just when students start a project, but also why they start at that specific time and if that starting time is a habit or if it depends on what they're writing about or in which class it is assigned. If these are your interests, it might be more effective to work with people (see Chapter 6) to develop an **interview protocol** or a **case-study** approach, methods that would require you to ask fewer people about their study habits but would allow you to develop a deeper understanding of each individual student's writing habits. One isn't necessarily better or worse. Like all research methods, each approach provides different data and different opportunities for analysis. It just depends on what you want to know.

Surveys, interviews—these might be methods with which you're familiar, but there are lots of other useful methods for working with people. You might want to understand student writing processes by looking at all of a particular student's writing for a given project. Instead of asking the student about her habits and working with **reported data**, or information that someone has told you, you might use a kind of **textual analysis** (we'll detail some varieties of this in Chapter 4) to read all of her notes and drafts for a particular project to better understand not just what she reports about her writing practices but how and what and when she *actually* writes in the lead up to a due date. Sometimes our perceptions of our actions differ than what we actually do, particularly in regard to writing habits, so collecting data that's not reported can be helpful. Or you might want to **observe** that student while she writes to notice how

---

Try This: Plan Your Own Writing Research Project (30 minutes)

What are your research questions about writing? Consider the examples we've given and develop your own questions on the topic, then think about possible methods you can use to investigate those questions:

1. List your interests in and questions about writing and the research process.

2. Identify one area of interest on your list and develop it into an effective research question (a question that does not have a yes/no answer, one that requires primary research to answer).

3. Consider what methods might be appropriate to help you answer the question you have identified.

often she takes breaks, if she texts while she writes, or if she listens to music. You might ask her to take pictures of herself or her writing environment at different points during the writing process, and you might develop a comparative **visual analysis** of the images (see Chapter 7).

Research Example: Access to Clean Water

Here's an example of how to develop a research plan. Imagine you're interested in developing a project about water, a topic that has been in the news quite a bit as of late. Depending on your specific interest and the kind of data you are interested in collecting and working with, you can design very different research proposals:

- **If you want to work with sources,** maybe you'll select developing a "worknet" as a research method (see Chapter 3). Your work with sources would find a focal article to generate a radial diagram as you select and highlight connections. One emerging connection, such as a linkage between long-term health outcomes and access to water filtration systems, can begin to crystalize as a research question that guides you in seeking and finding further sources or in choosing other methods appropriate to pairing with the question.

- **If you want to work with word**s (see Chapter 4), maybe you'll select content analysis as a research method to make sense of the discourse you find on your local water treatment plant's website. You might find that there is specialized or technical language, such as multiple mentions of contamination of which you were not aware, or terms with which you are unfamiliar (e.g., acidity, PPM, or pH). Gathering these terms and beginning to investigate their meanings can serve as the genesis of an emerging research focus.

- **If you want to work with people** (see Chapter 5), maybe you'll select survey as a research method, and you'll distribute a survey about drinking water to everyone in your classes, perhaps asking questions about their uses of water fountains and bottle refill stations or their knowledge about where their water comes from. You may learn that folks in your community have not had consistent access to potable water.

- **If you want to work with places and things** (see Chapter 6), maybe you'll select site observation as a research method, and you'll schedule a visit to your local water treatment plant. You may discover upon visiting that the plant is adjacent to a number of factories, or that it is difficult to access, perhaps that there is no one to give you a tour, or that much of the area is off limits. All of these on-site discoveries, carefully chronicled, substantiate distinctive ways of knowing not otherwise available.

- **If you want to work with images** (see Chapter 7), maybe you'll visit a local river, stream, or lake shore and photograph scenes where litter and wildlife are in close proximity, or where signs communicate about expectations for environmental care. A selection of such images may stand as a convincing set of visual evidence and may accompany a simple map identifying locations where you found problems or where additional signage is needed.

Try This: Brainstorming with Methods (30 minutes)

We've illustrated two examples, one focusing on the timing of student writing projects and another focusing on water. Now try this out on your own. Select an interest and work through how each of the methods listed would generate different data with the potential to draw different kinds of connections:

- Working with sources
- Working with words
- Working with people
- Working with places and things
- Working with images

As you consider an interest in light of each of these research methods, now would also be a good time to revisit the book's table of contents and then to turn to the chapters themselves to leaf around and begin to see the more specific and nuanced approaches to the methods under each heading.

The data you work with and the conclusions you can draw are dependent on the research method you select. Each approach provides particular insights into your topic and the world more broadly.

■ Research Across the Disciplines

Research conventions,* or the expectations about how research is conducted and written about, differ across the disciplines—whether that is theatre, mathematics, criminal justice, anthropology, etc. Some disciplines generally value quantitative data over qualitative data and vice versa. Many disciplines gravitate to certain methods and methodologies and specific patterns of writing up and citing data. Usually these conventions can be rhetorically traced to the values of a particular discipline. For instance, many humanities disciplines (English and World Languages, for instance) favor using MLA style to cite sources, and many social science disciplines (Psychology and Sociology, for instance) generally adhere to APA style. One of the primary differences in these citation styles is that MLA generally privileges author name and page number, which can be traced to the importance of specific wording at the heart of language study. APA privileges author name and year, which can be traced to the ways that social sciences value *when* something was published.

Citation conventions are one of the most concrete, visible differences that distinguish research across disciplines. But the differences are often much deeper and more abstract. How do you decide which method is appropriate for a particular research project? How do you make data meaningful in a particular context? The way you answer these questions constitutes your **research methodology**, or your thinking about a research project—and methodology, similar to citation style, usually demonstrates disciplinary values. Whether or not you *state* your methodology, everyone has a way of thinking about the method they choose and how the data they are using matters. Articulating a methodology simply makes that approach transparent to your audience and clear to yourself. Thus, a research methodology is the approach to a method, or the understanding and thinking that orga-

Research conventions adapt and change right along with the people who do research, the problems to which the research responds, and contemporary technologies.

nizes a particular method, as we show in Figure 1.1. Returning again to the etymology of "method" noted earlier (meta- and -hodos), consider the new part of the term, -ology. This addition assigns to method its reason for being selected. Accounting explicitly for the rationale, motives, and appropriateness of a research design, a methodology answers to justifications, underlying values, and established traditions for how knowledge is made and what kinds of knowledge matters in a given discipline.

For example, if you survey 100 people at your university about the timing of their writing projects, and you develop quantitative data as a result of your survey, you present that data as meaningful and suggest that such numbers provide a useful window into understanding student writing. However, you might not agree with this approach. You might think that to really understand student writing, you need to talk to students and ask open-ended questions. Or, you might believe that reported data about writing behaviors is *not* meaningful because we know that what people say they do and what they actually do are often very different things. You may believe that we need mixed methods to most effectively provide a portrait of student writing on campus, so you might design your study such that

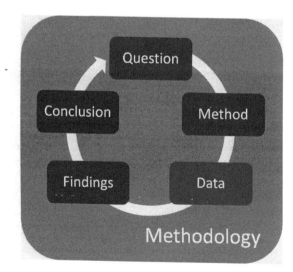

Figure 1.1. Components of methodology in research design.

you incorporate both survey and interview data. Ultimately the kind of data that methodology values is related to disciplinary values, and as you select a research project, a professional focus, and a profession, you will inherit disciplinary values. For example, researchers in the humanities might especially value qualitative data, and researchers in STEM fields might especially value quantitative data. As you become a more ingrained member of a disciplinary community (for instance when the major or job you take starts to feel familiar) we encourage you to keep questioning the methodology and values you inherit.

In Figure 1.2, we show how developing more questions along the way in all parts of your research design may give way to more complexity in your project.

Critical conversations about research are both **normative**, in that they usually bring together many scholars' thinking about a particular issue, and **disruptive**, in that new findings can up-end a particular conversation. Much of these changes are attributable to developments in methodology, such as updates in how we value a particular method or how we interpret certain findings. Changes to methodologies often cause significant ruptures in research communities. We are familiar with some of these large ruptures:

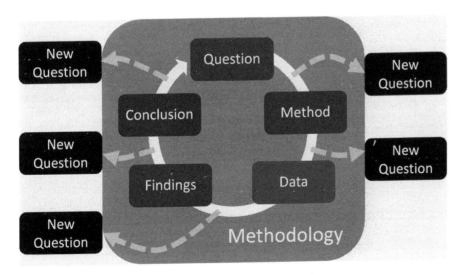

Figure 1.2. Complexity in research design.

the earth revolves around the sun instead of the reverse, bleeding a patient does not make her healthier, students learn most effectively through practice rather than listening by rote, etc. It is not always easy to come across findings that cause a rupture; however, as you examine the evolution of critical conversations over time, you might notice that they change slowly as new ruptures slowly become accepted in their associated communities.

■ Using Research Methods Ethically

The decisions you make in developing an effective research question, matching it to an appropriate research method, and then responsibly analyzing the implications of your findings (research design), are especially important because research is **subjective**. Subjectivity is often seen as negative and is frequently leveled as a reason to mistrust a decision or judgment, as in, "You're just being subjective." But: all research is subjective, all research is communication. Of course, not all scholars and fields believe this, but let us try to convince you, because it is important. This belief is central to conducting ethical research.

There is no pure objectivity when it comes to research. Research is conducted by people, all of whom have different ideas about effective research, but researchers abide by a code of ethics that holds them to standards that help them maintain safety and develop meaningful research. Even quantitative research, even computer algorithms that identify trends—all of the methods associated with developing this data are engineered by people and are, thus, subjective. And this is a good thing!

Instead of striving for **objective*** research (an impossibility), we strive for **ethical research**. Ethical research takes into account the fact that people perform research and that their research designs are impacted by their own **subjectivities**: the thoughts, beliefs, and values that make us human. As researchers, it is essential to be reflective on our subjectivities, mitigate subjectivities that might make us conduct research unfairly, and adhere to high ethical standards for research. We will spend more time working through these ethical considerations in Chapter 2.

You may think of objectivity as being defined as "without bias." Yet it is far more complex! Marianne Janack (2002) lists 13 different ways we might consider objectivity, from a scientific method, to disinterest, to rationality, to an attitude of "psychological distance" (275). What do you mean when you use the term "objective"?

■ Developing a Research Proposal

Much of what we've discussed in this chapter is about ideas and about how to approach research broadly. A tangible way to make sense of these ideas is by developing a research proposal. A proposal allows you to concretize your thinking about a project and receive feedback on your plan. This is a crucial step because an instructor, mentor, or peer might help you improve your research design and better align your question, method, and data to help you develop useful findings. A proposal is an inventional method, not a contract. As you learn more about your topic, you will most likely refine your research question, and you may even decide on a different method. In each chapter, we'll introduce further methods for invention and innovative ways to approach a research question, perhaps in ways you haven't before. One thing to keep in mind as you plan your research is how you may want to present your work (delivery) and who may be interested in your research (audience). Sometimes the research we do remains relatively private, but usually the purpose of research is to develop new knowledge and *share it*, as we discuss in Chapter 8. Spread the word, contribute to the critical conversation about the area in which you're interested so that others can test out your ideas, build on your ideas, and use the knowledge you've developed. Maintain this audience awareness throughout your research process, even from the beginning—it will impact how you design and deliver your work.

■ Focus on Delivery: Writing a Research Proposal

A research proposal is a stated plan for research, which may change, and some of which should change throughout the course of your project. This is a plan for your project, but as the saying goes, "the best laid plans…"

A research proposal should include the following:

- A clear articulation of your question;
- The critical conversation to which you hope your research contributes;

- Your chosen research method;
- The basic methodology that guides your choice of method;
- Plans for how you will make sense of your data.

You should not have a thesis or a conclusion. Since you haven't done the research yet, this would be impossible.

Instead, allow your proposal to be exploratory, and make sure that it is interesting to you, that you're asking a question that you actually want to know the answer to. This small step is crucial to developing an engaging, thoughtful project. If you're not interested in the question you pose, keep asking questions, keep inventing until you come upon something you care about. If you struggle with this process, reach out to an instructor, mentor, or peer; talking to someone else is one of the simplest and most generative inventional opportunities around!

■ Works Cited

Burke, Kenneth. *The Philosophy of Literary Form.* University of California Press, 1974.

Janack, Marianne. "Dilemmas of Objectivity." *Social Epistemology: A Journal of Knowledge, Culture and Policy*, vol. 16, no. 3, 2002, pp. 267–281. *Taylor & Francis Online*, doi.org/10.1080/0269172022000025624.

Chapter 2. Making Research Ethical

"[E]very methods-based decision is also an ethical decision."

—Heidi McKee

He wrote a juicy memoir claiming the discovery of the DNA double helix model as his own, casting aspersions on his long-time collaborators.

After she got the results back from her DNA testing kit, she learned of a family predisposition for a genetic disorder that she had passed down to her children unknowingly.

The ancestry software he purchased showed a direct family connection to infamous slave-owners.

They named the genetically cloned sheep Dolly after Dolly Parton, for pretty tawdry reasons.

Although she ran an organic farm, she often found that genetically modified seeds made their way into her fields, distributed by winds from nearby farms.

The brief anecdotes that begin this chapter constitute just some of the ethical quandaries resulting from what some have termed "The Birth of Molecular Biology," the development of the DNA double helix model. This important scientific finding was peopled with unethical behavior and scandal, and the many resulting questions that have arisen from the discovery continue to churn both inside of and external to the scientific community: Should DNA be modified? For food? For people? For sheep? What about ancestry software and genetic testing? Who should have access to genetic data, and what should they be allowed to do with it? Such ethical considerations are an important component of this research project. Consider the following questions that help address ethical issues when conducting research:

- How is research developed and by whom?
- How are data and participants treated and protected during the research process?

- Who claims credit for the work conducted? Who cites others as collaborators and forebears of their work?
- Is research written about intimately, distantly, in first person, in third person?
- How is data stored? Who has access to data?
- Who benefits or is hurt by research?

All of these questions (and more!) make up the ethical component of research design. Understanding research ethics and wrestling with the often complex questions that the ethical component of research design entails are essential elements of conducting effective, responsible research. **Research ethics** address the evolving conventions, codes of conduct, and standards research communities adopt to strive for ethical development and circulation of research and to protect audiences, authors, and their research contributions.

■ Ethical Approaches to Research

The scientific method, which is often the foundation for much of our understanding about the research process, asks us to strive for objectivity. This is a **positivist** approach to research that assumes that there is one clear answer to a research question. However, in contemporary contexts, and certainly in the example of the development of the double helix DNA model, most scholars have agreed that research is rarely so clear cut. There are usually multiple answers to research questions—some better, some more conventional, some more accepted by **communities of practice** than others. This lack of certainty can sometimes worry apprentice researchers; they might be concerned that any answer is right or that research is more about saying the right thing rather than striving for answers. This is not the case! It just means that in this **constructivist** world of research—an understanding of research that considers the interactions between researchers, research subjects, and their environments—our goal is not objectivity but fairness and an ethical approach to research.

Further, some researchers suggest that the goal of research is **strong objectivity**, an orientation toward research that acknowledges the role of people in developing research and encourages researchers to acknowledge their own **subjectivities**, or the potential biases and experiences that might impact their approach to research design and data analysis.*

■ Ethos is Collective and Individual

We often reduce **ethos** to considering whether a particular author is credible, but ethos is largely collective. Pause for a moment and consider where and why you're reading this text. Most likely you've selected a place to sit and read because of a combination of reasons related to convenience, access, necessity, and reputation. Let's focus on the latter in particular. If you're reading at work, a coffee shop, or at home, you may have chosen this place because you've talked with others about the right place to study, or you might have taken friends and family's advice because you trust them. You're reading this book because you're in a class at an institution that values your experiences with writing, and your instructor has selected a text based on many factors, including its reputable publisher and authors who actively conduct research on the subject area. So even though you may be sitting alone with a book, there are many people who stand behind you, impacting the decisions you make and your broader credibility as a student and learner. And even though the names of only three authors appear on this book, there are hundreds of friends, family members, scholars, publishers, and editors who have contributed to the content and collective ethos of this book.

It goes deeper: your instructor has an impact on your ethos, just as you have an impact on them. If you do well in the class, it suggests that she is a good instructor. This might impact her status at the university, her qualification for a potential promotion, or her standing in the department. If you mention down the road that you had this particular instructor, someone else may expect that you're a good writer because you have had good instruction, and they may hire you for an internship or job, or maybe they'll ask you to complete a challenging project because your instructor has contributed to your ethos as an effective writer. Your classmates impact your ethos, and you theirs. If your classmates are effective writers in their careers post-gradua-

Accepting that research is complex and that there are no easy, clear answers makes the research process more honest, more exciting, more effective, and, ironically, less biased.

Although we often boil down questions of ethos to individuals, they are just one access point in a network of ethos that is largely collective and constantly shifting and circulating.

tion, graduates from your university may gain a reputation for being particularly well-qualified for careers in communication. This could impact your prospects when you graduate, and your performance will impact students who graduate after you as well. Your college or university impacts your **ethos.*** And the network continues.

When you decide that a particular author is credible and has a reliable ethos, it's because a network of people have helped establish that—the journal in which they have published, the institutions and organizations to which they belong, their partners and families, etc.

■ Ethics and Secondary Research

As we noted in the introduction, many of our recommendations in this book oscillate between recommendations for **invention**—developing access points

---

Try This: Consider What Activities and People Impact Your Ethos (30 minutes)

You have had a long history as a reader and writer. The people, places, and activities with which you have come into contact during this history impact your ethos.

Compose a drawing that illustrates the network of influences that collectively constitute your ethos. You may hand-sketch or use clip-art, stick figures, and/or text to develop your composition. The goal is to make tangible the collective nature of your own ethos so that you can consider how this principle extends to other researchers. Consider the following invention questions to help develop your composition:

- What are your earliest reading and writing experiences? Who and what contributed?
- What was the first primary research project you conducted (think of "research" broadly— any time you test a theory or answer a question for yourself, you're doing a form of primary research)? Who influenced the research?
- Who has taught you about conducting research? What are the primary lessons you've learned?
- What formal school and learning experiences impact your approach to research?
- What experiences external to school impact your approach to research?

for your research project, or what some refer to, in part, as prewriting or brainstorming—and **delivery**—the ways in which your research project is communicated, or delivered, to an audience. An ethical approach to research should impact both invention and delivery in relation to your project. A starting place for many research projects includes the invention associated with identifying secondary research that informs your project. Chapter 3: Worknets provides a specific framework for reading sources deeply. In particular, we describe four methods, or phases, for reading secondary research. The first phase is the **semantic** phase, which asks you to be attentive to keywords in the text you've selected. The second phase is the **bibliographic** phase, which asks you to trace intersections between sources. The third phase is the **affinity** phase, which invites you to consider how writers are connected to each other. And finally, the fourth phase, the **choric** phase, asks you to consider the broader rhetorical context in which an article is written. Before you delve into this framework in detail, consider how secondary research that forms a **critical conversation** about an issue is constructed. In this section we'll also work to identify how to establish ethos, evaluate texts and authors, and learn citation systems, processes associated with an ethical approach to secondary research.

■ Establishing Ethos

One of the primary ways that researchers demonstrate their understanding of research convention and establish **ethos** is by carefully citing the authors they've read who have contributed to the critical conversation they'd like to join. **Ethos** is an author's credibility, or the trust an author establishes with an audience, and it can be a measure of how much **uptake,*** or interest, influence, and sharing, their work gets once they've completed a research project. When researching your area of interest, knowing what a particular community has said about it and finding the niche or gap in the research about it provides an opportunity for you to make a contribution to this conversation. Thoroughly reading secondary sources and genuinely representing others' ideas is part of an ethical approach to secondary research that helps establish your ethos and that may pave the way for you to add your voice in ways that are important to a

Although uptake sounds nebulous, you can see it in action every time someone on social media shares a particular message, meme, or visual.

given community. Chapter 3 helps demonstrate an ethical level of engagement with which researchers should consider secondary sources.

For instance, one of our former students, Gabriel Green, collaborated on a research project that considered the impact of campus crime and safety alerts. The project started with a question that we shared—how do the safety alerts impact the campus community? He engaged in primary research, gathering university records of crime alerts since the beginning of their circulation. He also considered secondary research, the critical conversation surrounding on-campus safety. By effectively citing experts in the field to demonstrate his knowledge of the current, existing discussion, he was able to establish ethos and craft an engaging exigency, or timely reason, to situate the research.

Demonstrating understanding of critical conversations and research conventions is key to establishing ethos, but having personal experience related to an issue can also make a researcher particularly well-suited for a particular

---

Try This: Making an Argument for Your Research by Identifying an Opening (1 hour)

Effective research proposals (Chapter 1) spotlight for readers how the researcher is connected to the work of others. Such gestures can deepen the researcher's ethos because they acknowledge that this new work bears relation to what has preceded it. Based on his work examining how scholars introduce research projects by demonstrating a gap in the critical conversation, John Swales developed a model to show apprentice researchers to do the same. Swales observed that scholars make the following basic moves:

- **Name the critical conversation.** This might include scholarly discussions of strategies for success in university writing, ethical considerations for the research process, concerns about the financial stability of a particular institution, etc.
- **Identify threads or themes related to the research area.** In this step, writers narrow their focus and cite authors their work draws from and to which they hope to respond.
- **Articulate what has not been said before** and explain why it is important that we consider this particular aspect of the issue.
- **State their argument** and demonstrate its importance in contributing to the identified opening in the research conversation.

Try it out for the secondary research you do!

project. Student researcher Zepher Barber developed a project about the best ways for students to prepare for first-year writing and to acclimate to the university. Because she was a successful, experienced, first-year student herself, Ms. Barber was an especially effective researcher to develop such a project. By claiming her status as a first-year student, and thus her privileged proximity to the area of research that she was writing about, she helped establish her ethos. Ethos is thus emplaced: it is related to the "where" of a writing situation, the "who" conducting the research, and the "when" that animates the experience.

■ Evaluating Texts and Authors

When you approach an article, you want to consider the venue and the authors' collective ethos. If you search for **peer-reviewed** secondary research through a library database, research that has been considered and shared by a community of experts, this technology helps you identify credible sources. Database searches often (though not always) filter out sources that have not been verified as credible by peers within a research community. But why is peer review so important? Why are peer-reviewed sources often privileged over other types of sources? It helps to know how the peer review process works.

Consider this textbook. Before this book got to you, it went through a long peer review and editorial process in which multiple people reviewed the work and provided feedback. This process is demonstrated in Figure 2.1. We first developed a book proposal, which went to the publisher. It then went out for peer review to eight experts in the field, writing teachers from all kinds of universities and colleges. They provided feedback, and we developed a draft of the book based on those reviews. Then we sent the complete draft to our editor, received feedback from her, made changes, and then chapters of the book were again sent to expert peer reviewers. The whole process took a few years!

Journal articles are a little different. Once you complete the research and write the article, you send it to a journal. The editor decides whether the article is appropriate to send out for review by asking questions like the following: Are these authors credible? Do they use evidence to support their claims? Are

Authors Drafting	12 months
Authors Revising	3 months
Editors Reviewing	3 months
Authors Revising	3 months
External Peer Review	3 months
Authors Revising	2 months
Copyediting & Production	2 months
Final Review	1 month

Figure 2.1. The development and review process for this book.

they arguing something totally wacky and empirically wrong? If the editor decides it is appropriate to do so, she sends the chapter to at least two experts in the field, and any of the authors' identifying aspects are removed so that they are anonymous. The reviewers decide whether the article is appropriate for publication and whether the authors should make any changes. This part of the process usually takes at least a year.

So why bother? Why engage in such a long process? The time, multiple perspectives, opportunities for revision and reflection, and multiple layers of review help ensure that the ideas that are shared represent rigorous, effective, and ethical research. Peer review ensures that there are multiple experts who vouch for the ideas shared, and in this way the article shares the collective ethos of the community who has engaged with the work. This is in contrast to a newspaper article, which usually has at least one other person who has read the work, and a blog or independent website, in which the author may be the only one who has read and reviewed the material. This doesn't mean that information from other sources is incorrect; it just means that you have to be even more careful about considering the ethos of the author and article because the peer review process hasn't helped do that for you. You are forced to rely more on the author's individual ethos rather than consider the collective ethos that is communicated through peer review.

Especially if your project requires that you do research outside of peer-reviewed venues (and there are lots of good reasons for this!), you might ask the following questions of the sources with which you engage (and make sure to visit Chapter 3, which provides a framework for working deeply with sources):

- What are the authors' relationship to the area of research?

- What credentials do they have that help establish their expertise in this area?

- Do the authors have any subjectivities that might compromise their ability to develop credible research?

Remember, providing an opinion or having subjectivities does not mean that an author lacks credibility.* You just have to consider how honest an author is about those opinions and subjectivities and whether they let their values and beliefs compromise their ability to do ethical research. These considerations function in everyday life, too. If someone invites you to a restaurant they own and tells you that it's the best restaurant in town, you might question their ability to make an informed opinion. They have a vested, economic interest in you visiting their restaurant. However, if a friend eats at that restaurant every week and tells you it's the best restaurant in town, you might take their opinion more seriously. They have a clear opinion, and they're subjective about the restaurant (they love it!), but their ideas aren't compromised by their relationship to the restaurant. If you hear from multiple friends whose opinions you respect that it's the best restaurant around, you'll probably plan to go check it out. All of this is to say, awareness of an author's opinion or subjectivity doesn't mean that an article is not credible. Folks who are honest about their subjectivities should actually be viewed as potentially more credible than others who aren't aware of how their experiences impact their approach to research.

All people have opinions and subjectivities; it is essentially the definition of being human—subjectivities are inescapable.

■ Learning Citation Systems

Once you've selected effective articles and spent time with them, how do you cite them in your research project? And why should you cite them? Citing sources provides a breadcrumb pathway for your audience so they can follow the research path you've taken, make their own judgments about what you've found, and perhaps disagree with your findings or add to what you've contributed. You demonstrate your ethos as a credible, ethical researcher by correctly citing research and being attentive to the conventions of research practice. Unfortunately, citations are often talked about as simply a vehicle to avoid plagiarism, but we hope that you'll move beyond such a perspective. Citations are important because they're trail markers or signposts on the research path. You put them down so that both you and your audience remember where you've traversed. Because research—when it's good, when it's engaging—is quite a ride. It takes you to unexpected places, and if you don't leave clear trail markers, it is very possible to get lost. Further, research is a conversation between you and the other researchers you're citing and drawing on in the project you've developed. When you cite, you highlight the different voices in the project. This multiple voicing is indicative of how we communicate. We always bring other people's ideas into our communication, both written and spoken. This characteristic of communication is known as **intertextuality**, a concept that describes how other people's language is seamlessly embedded in our own. Citation celebrates this natural aspect of communication and makes it visible.

There are many different citation systems. Communities in the humanities often use Modern Language Association (MLA) style. Social science research communities often use American Psychological Association (APA) style. Many STEM fields have citation styles that are specific to individual journals or subdisciplines. Other disciplines use a version of Chicago Style. It can be easy to feel that citations are arbitrary, but when you look at them closely and alongside each other, the differences and conventions become more meaningful. In fact, the conventions function as clues to what a particular discipline values and what kind of sources they use most.* This is part of why citation styles are updated so frequently; disciplinary values grow and change, particularly as the kinds of evidence they cite changes.

Every choice—to include an author's full name or use their initial instead, to capitalize every word in an article title (or not!), to italicize or abbreviate, to use a comma, period, or semicolon, or even to emphasize the placement of the year of publication—is meaningful and has reasons behind it.

Consider the style variations in Figures 2.2, 2.3, and 2.4 of a single citation that represents an article we read to inform the beginning of this chapter:

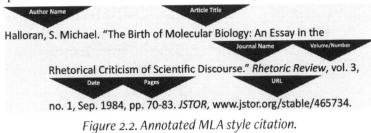

Figure 2.2. Annotated MLA style citation.

MLA style: Halloran, S. Michael. "The Birth of Molecular Biology: An Essay in the Rhetorical Criticism of Scientific Discourse." *Rhetoric Review*, vol. 3, no. 1, Sep. 1984, pp. 70–83. *JSTOR*, www.jstor.org/stable/465734.

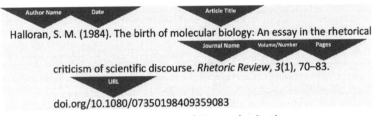

Figure 2.3. Annotated APA style citation.

APA style: Halloran, S. M. (1984). The birth of molecular biology: An essay in the rhetorical criticism of scientific discourse. *Rhetoric Review, 3*(1), 70–83. https://doi.org/10.1080/07350198409359083

Try This: Comparing Citation Systems (30 minutes)

1. Locate a peer-reviewed source that aligns with your research interests.
2. Cite the source using different citation systems.
3. Next, compare citations, and examine them rhetorically.
   a. What are the differences?
   b. Consider, how does citation demonstrate disciplinary values?
   c. How can order and punctuation be rhetorical and meaningful?

Figure 2.4. Annotated Chicago style citation.

Chicago style: Halloran, S. Michael. 1984. "The Birth of Molecular Biology: An Essay in the Rhetorical Criticism of Scientific Discourse." *Rhetoric Review* 3, no. 1 (September): 70–83. https://doi.org/10.1080/07350198409359083.

You do not have to memorize a particular citation system, because it will inevitably change as research conventions change. Instead, try to understand the citation system that you use most frequently. Consider the components and think through the relationship of this citation system to the disciplinary values that you see reflected.*

If you work towards making sense of the citation systems rather than just committing to memory where the various commas go, it will make more sense to you and you will be more flexible in moving between citation styles if necessary. It will also be less confusing when you have to update to a new version of the citation system.

■ Ethics and Primary Research

In subsequent chapters we will address numerous research methods for working with words (Chapter 4), people (Chapter 5), places and things (Chapter 6), and visuals (Chapter 7). Each set of methods requires different thinking when it comes to ethics, but many of these considerations are related to the impact research has on people, the safety of their environment, and the potential benefits or detriments to their privacy.

■ Working with Human Subjects

When you conduct primary research with human subjects (which might include texts, images, or places) you need to take into account particular ethical aspects of your research. Imagine if the scientists who discovered the DNA Double Helix had considered how their discovery might impact subsequent generations. What if they had suggested guidelines? Or, what if they hadn't fought over ownership of the model? How might their interactions with each other have changed ethical approaches to the treatment of DNA data? Nowadays, universities have **Institutional Review Boards (IRB)** that approve and make recommendations about research with human subjects. If you do not intend to publish your research, your research is not necessarily replicable, or it won't contribute to *generalized knowledge*—conversations about research to which particular communities and bodies of research orient, then you do not necessarily need to have your research plan approved by an IRB. When in doubt, you can always ask a faculty member or contact your IRB representative to see if your work is exempt. Even if your research need not be approved by IRB, it is useful to consider their recommendations for ethical research with human subjects because these regulations were developed to protect people. Unfortunately, all of these regulations were developed because researchers have conducted incredibly unethical research. Joseph Breault and other scholars have detailed how our current guidelines have come to be. In brief, many of our guidelines are a version of the 1976 Belmont Report, a report developed by a commission, the purpose of which was to ensure **informed consent** and **ethical treatment** of research participants. Informed consent is required when you are conducting research with human subjects. This just means that you ensure that the person you are surveying or interviewing (see Chapter 5 for detailed focus on research methods designed for working with people) fully understands the research in which they're taking part and that they agree to participate. It is important to let participants know what the research is about; if there will be any benefits, danger, or threat to them; and that they can choose not to participate at any time.

Informed consent and recommendations for ethical treatment of human subjects is a response to inhumane research conducted by Nazis on people during World War II. There have been other problematic, unethical studies—too many to mention here—but one particularly heinous, well-known study is the Tuskegee Study in which African American men infected with syphilis went untreated for forty years so that researchers could examine the impact of the disease. Subsequent regulations ensure that research does not hurt participants and that participants are fully aware of what a study in which they take part fully entails.

This notion of informed consent is central to ethical treatment of research participants. Folks need to fully understand what they are agreeing to when you ask them to participate in your research. There are some populations of people—children, prisoners, mentally disabled persons, and pregnant women—who receive additional protections according to IRB protocols, so you might take this into account if your research includes members of one of these groups. Further, face-to-face research with people can differ from research that you conduct in digital spaces. For instance, if you conduct an informal poll through social media for the purposes of a research project, it may not feel like you're doing research, but you are! You will need to get consent from your participants, though it might look different than obtaining consent in person.

■ Interacting with Audiences

The thing is, even if you don't set out to interview or survey folks, your research still might involve interaction with people, and ultimately, the goal of research is to share your ideas with an audience. If you're taking photographs as part of

---

Try This: Learn About Your Institution's IRB Office (30 minutes)

Every institution has their own IRB office, complete with their own guidelines and reporting structures. To get a sense of your institution's ethical approach to research, find your IRB office's website, and consider the following:

- Who is on your institution's IRB board? Are they faculty members? Staff members? What disciplines do they represent?
- What is the process on your campus for conducting research with human subjects?
- Are there different expectations for undergraduate student, graduate student, faculty member, and staff member researchers?
- How does your institution define research with human subjects? How does it define ethics?

You might also identify a nearby institution or a school you considered attending. Find its IRB office website and compare it with the one at your school. Where are the overlaps? What is different? And what is the significance of the comparisons you have made?

your research, as you'll spend time with in Chapter 7, you'll have to consider whether or not people will end up in those images. And if so, do they know they're being photographed? If you're doing textual research on a blog or a Facebook community, even though the texts you're considering are public, folks might not think of that space as public. You'll need to think through how you interact with your potential research participants, data, and audience.

For instance, Kate is currently conducting a project that examines the impact of plagiarism accusations on students and faculty members. All people in her study are asked to consent to participate in the study. However, in talking to research participants about their experiences, she has learned about other students who have plagiarized. What is Kate's responsibility as a researcher in writing about these people who have plagiarized but who have not consented to participate in her study? As a researcher, she needs to consider the expectations for student privacy, the sensitivity of the material, and the potential harms and/or benefits to the university community. Can she anonymize the students in the stories she has heard, or would sharing any part of these narratives cause the students to suffer? Key aspects to consider when making such decisions are the relationship between the researcher and the research population—or **proximity**—and potential **beneficence***of the research. In this case, Kate is a faculty member, and her research participants are students, so although they all interact in the same sphere, there is a power differential that complicates the relationship. The findings of Kate's research have significantly beneficial potential for the university, but not at the expense of outing students who have not shared their plagiarism stories publicly.

Beneficence asks whether the research is charitable, equitable, and fair to participants by taking into full account the possible consequences for the researcher and the participants.

■ Designing Writing That Does Ethical Work

Hopefully you are already on board with the importance of approaching research ethically, with ethics and fairness as your primary research objective rather than objectivity. If you still have questions, or if you're not sold on these ideas yet, please don't hesitate to talk to your instructor and colleagues (and us!) about your questions, engage in your own research on ethics, and see the end of this chapter for further reading recommendations. But if you are ready to start designing ethical research, some important written products to develop are **research protocols**, or your plan for research; **scripts**, or the particular way you will describe your research to participants, particularly for focus groups in which a group of people participate in the research or

---

Try This Together: Considering Ethical Research (45 minutes)

In groups, consider the following situations, which include complex ethical components from research projects scholars have developed. Talk through the ethical issues at hand: how might you handle them?

- In 2012, scholar Jody Shipka bought six boxes from a yard sale that included personal photographs, diaries, and scrapbooks from a couple she did not know. These boxes inspired her project, "Inhabiting Dorothy," in which she attempted to travel and record the same paths that the couple had catalogued in their materials. Dr. Shipka invited audience members to also participate in the project, reenacting experiences and images of folks they do not know. What are the ethical components at work here?

- Technical Communication Scholar Fernando Sanchez examined a 2017 court case in response to gerrymandering in two Texas districts. He examined the ways that legislative mapmakers used GIS software to create maps that make political arguments. How might maps and their representations of people represent ethical or unethical research practices? How do images and their representation impact audiences? How might subsequent researchers take up Sanchez's findings?

- Heidi McKee described how in 2008 she read a research project that accidentally included contact information for one of the research participants who was supposed to be anonymous. The authors had included a screen capture of a newspaper article that described the research participant's brush with the law. Although the researchers meant to keep the subject's identity secret, the screen capture was easily enlarged, and the article and identifying information about the person was easily accessed. How does this experience highlight the complexities of maintaining research participant anonymity? How does digital research and publication impact this complexity?

- Photographer Christine Rogers developed a series of images between 2007 and 2008 titled "New Family" in which she posed for family photos (complete with the quintessential hand on shoulder pose) with people who were strangers to her. In what ways would Ms. Rogers have to approach participants? What are the ethical considerations of such a project?

there are multiple research facilitators; and **participation** or **consent forms**. Below, we'll focus in particular on developing a participation form, which is necessary for conducting research with human subjects. In Chapter 5, we outline specific research methods for working with people, including surveys, interviews, and case studies, but before you do that work, you'll need to make sure that participants understand and want to participate in your research.

Often in working with human subjects, we are asked to "do no harm" and to weigh the potential benefit to society in relation to the potential discomfort to research participants. We hope that this chapter helps demonstrate why it is so important (and complicated) to consider ethical questions in conducting secondary research and designing primary research, but we invite you to go a step further. In the chapters that follow, you'll be introduced to multiple research methods and invited to develop invention activities for potential research projects. Instead of merely considering how to avoid harm, consider how your research might actually do good. How can we use these research methods to not just perform ethical research but to in fact be more ethical?

Focus on Delivery: Composing a Participation Form

The primary purpose of a participation or consent form is to ensure that research participants understand what is being asked of them if they choose to participate in your research so that they can fully and knowledgeably consent (or choose not to consent). However, designing such a form is also important invention work. Thinking through and writing down what participation in your study entails helps you think through what you're asking participants to do, and it might help you revise and reconceive your project in productive ways.

If you plan to publish your research (or you even just think you might want to), if your research is replicable, if your research will contribute to generalizable knowledge, or if you would like to work with protected populations, you will need IRB approval for your research. Each IRB is a little different, and they offer recommended templates as part of their resources for authors.

If your research does not require IRB approval, your form may include many of the same components that IRB templates include, but the structure may change depending on your project needs and interests. Your participation form should address the following aspects of the research project:

- What, in detail, does your research entail?

- What will research participants be asked to do?

- Are there any risks or potential benefits to participants? Risks are pretty obvious for medical research, but don't forget that research about writing can also elicit discomfort and potential risk for participants. Consider whether your research might make someone uncomfortable. Might your research have the potential to reveal something personal regarding their sexuality, gender, citizenship, religion, etc.?

- Explain what product will be created out of the research—who will the audience for that product be and in what venue will the findings be shared?

- Will the research participants remain anonymous? Do you want them to have the option to be anonymous or not? Perhaps they'll want credit for the ideas they've shared with you.

- Will research participants have an opportunity to comment on drafts of the research or view the completed project?

Finally, make sure to give your research participants an out, meaning—let them know that they don't have to participate and that they can choose to not participate at any time. This includes after the research is complete! Any time before research is published, participants should have your contact information so that they can let you know if they change their minds.

■ Works Cited

Breault, Joseph L. "Protecting Human Research Subjects: The Past Defines the Future." *The Ochsner Journal*, vol. 6, no. 1, 2006, pp. 15–20. *PubMed Central*, www.ncbi.nlm.nih.gov/pmc/articles/PMC3127481/.

Halloran, S. Michael. "The Birth of Molecular Biology: An Essay in the Rhetorical Criticism of Scientific Discourse." *Rhetoric Review*, vol. 3, no. 1, Sep. 1984, pp. 70–83. *JSTOR*, www.jstor.org/stable/465734.

McKee, Heidi. A. "Ethical and Legal Issues for Writing Researchers in an Age of Media Convergence." *Computers and Composition*, vol. 25, no. 1, 2008, pp. 104–22, doi.org/10.1016/j.compcom.2007.09.007.

Rogers, Christine. *New Family*. www.cerogers.net/work/new-family.

Sánchez, Fernando. 2018. "Racial Gerrymandering and Geographic Information Systems: Subverting the 2011 Texas District Map with Election Technologies." *Technical Communication,* vol. 65, no. 4, 2018, 354-370.

Shipka, Jody. "On Estate Sales, Archives, and the Matter of Making Things." In *Provocations: Reconstructing the Archive*. cccdigitalpress.org/book/reconstructingthe archive/shipka.html.

Swales, John. M. *Genre Analysis: English in Academic and Research Settings*. Cambridge UP, 1990.

Chapter 3. Working with Sources: Worknets and Invention

To work with materials successfully, practitioners in many fields study how something is made. They may turn to instructions and diagrams, or they may take apart and put back together equipment. They may follow steps essential to understanding better how things fit together, which parts of a system are dependent on which other parts, and how—when things go well—the system operates.

For example, a materials engineer at a bicycle manufacturer may look at other models or even collect samples of bicycles and take them for a ride. The materials engineer might ponder, alone or in consultation with others, alternatives for any individual part or material necessary to the bike's functioning. She might take notes, draw and scribble about connections, or make mock-up prototypes.

In another comparable scenario, a pizza maker might follow a dough recipe several times before making a change to an essential component, such as trying a new oil or yeast or flour, or perhaps modifying resting time or the kneading process. The ingredients and process are both built up intricately and periodically unbuilt to ensure great familiarity with how things work.

Writing researchers frequently read, study, and consult sources as a way to stay apprised of new knowledge as well as long-established histories relevant to their questions. Sources are tremendously important among the materials writing researchers work with.

The reason researchers cite sources is simple: to establish credibility—build their ethos—writers have to show that they are members of their academic communities. They do this by pointing to other writers who have had, and are having, the research conversation they are interested in joining. You'll notice as you read any academic article that it usually begins with a **literature review**, or a synthesis of sources that shows explicitly that the writer knows the main arguments, or critical conversation, circulating about a particular topic and is then able to carve out a space for their own research question. But what can citing sources *do* for you? Here are some possibilities:

- It recognizes the history of how sources build on each other by relating new research to past research (homage; timeliness of current research).

- It lends credibility to the author—you!—who, by referencing sources, demonstrates care, ethics, rigor, and knowledge (authority; credibility).

- It revisits claims, data, and key concepts that serve as a foundation to the new research (build-up).

- It positions new research in relationship to the research gaps that it highlights (differentiation).

It's not enough, in working with a topic—say, climate change—to simply know it is of interest to a variety of scholars. A writer needs to become familiar with the key terms used by the scholarly community working on climate research, such as *greenhouse gas* and *carbon threshold*, and the historic data that is fundamental to that research. This might be represented by, for example, how the measurements of carbon levels in the atmosphere that have been taken by the National Oceanic and Atmospheric Administration at the Moana Loa Observatory since 1958 led to noticing that we have surpassed the 400 PPM, or parts per million, carbon threshold that is key to human thinking about climate change. Learning these things allows you to write your way into a complex topic and shows that you know enough to join the conversation.

But how do you begin? This chapter helps you begin to invent ideas by engaging deeply with sources. Seeking and finding appropriate sources and knowing them well enough to incorporate them into your writing is slow work. It can be especially slowed down when you are at the beginning, finding your way into an unfamiliar conversation for the first time. It takes time to trace even a sample of the relations that reach through and across sources.

In this chapter, we focus on one way that you can work with a text, or **source**, through working with the webs of relationships that extend out from it, or its web of connections with other sources. We call this kind of working with multiple texts **sourcework**, and it can show itself in a variety of ways—often through library research, keyword searches, paging through a source's bibliography or Works Cited page, or following a trail of online links or even a hunch about a key idea. Yet sourcework takes time, and that's something many student writers don't have a lot of when they are trying to navigate a complex topic and key details of a nuanced argument—all from one source! Given the time it takes to work with sources effectively, here we introduce you to a method of sourcework that we call **worknets**, a four-part model of working your way through one source such that it leads you towards other sources and ideas that will be useful to the thinking and framing of your project.

■ The Power of Worknets

Worknets give us a visual model for understanding how sources interrelate, how key words and ideas become attached to certain people, and why *provenance*—when something was written and where it came from—matters. At the center of any worknet is the source that you or your instructor sees as focal to the conversations happening in your research. Radiating outward from that source, as spokes from a wheel, are what we call nodal connections. Each nodal connection gives you another research path to follow and another way to connect with your source more deeply and less superficially. Often students are called upon to "incorporate five or seven or x sources" as though this is a quick and easy task—it isn't! But when you can treat a central source as one that leads you in a series of directions, each with its own path toward another source, concept, person, or event, you are more likely to read the whole thing. This will help you understand sources more fully, investigate what you don't understand, and more easily locate another source. It will also help you gather sources together and see how they connect to each other and what gaps in the sources emerge, which helps you piece together a literature review with your research question front and center.

Worknets provide you with a method for working within and across academic sources. As a way of helping you "invent" what you have to say, worknets

In terms of delivery, a complete worknet project can stand alone, it can serve as a useful building block for an annotation that is part of a larger annotated bibliography, or it can function as a starting point for a literature review.

are a source-based way of helping you to generate a path for your research that points you toward a particular question, gap, or needed extension of what has come before. A finished worknet consists of four phases: a **semantic** phase, which looks at significant words and phrases repeated in the text; a **bibliographic** phase, which connects your central or focal source to the other works the author has cited in her piece; an **affinity** phase, which shows how personal relationships shape sourcework; and a **choric** phase, which allows researchers to freely associate historic and sociocultural connections to the central source text.* After developing a finished worknet, which involves all four phases placed visually together, you will have many openings for further

---

Try This: Summarizing a Central Source (1 hour)

Return to the research proposal that you generated in Chapter 1 or "Making an Argument for Your Research" in Chapter 2. Spend some time coming up with key terms or phrases that succinctly capture your research interests, practicing with Boolean operators such as *and, or,* and *not* (e.g., "trees and diseases and campus"; "texting or IM and depression"; "composition and grades not music"). Begin with your library's databases in your major and, using these key terms, start narrowing your search to academic articles (rather than reviews, newspaper articles, or web pages, for example) using these key terms. Skim at least five sources as you look for your central source, taking notes on the following:

- What is the purpose of the research article?
- What methods did the researchers use to answer their research question?
- What did the researchers find out?
- What is the significance of the research?
- What research still needs to be done?

Taking these notes will allow you to see if the source you've read really connects with your curiosities and research direction. They also clearly lay out the basis of most academic articles: a hypothesis (the research question), methods (the tools used to answer a research question), results (what you found out), and discussion (why it matters). Putting these together in 50-100 words allows you to generate a **summary** of the key points of an academic article, letting you select the article that is the most interesting and central to your research question to begin your worknets.

research, and you will have gained a handle on the central source such that incorporating it into your writing via direct quotation, paraphrase, or summary is easier for you to achieve and more interesting for an audience to read. Worknets can follow the proposal you developed in Chapter 1, or they can offer you a method for reading sources that supports your drafting and refining a research focus and related proposal.

To develop a worknet, begin by selecting a researched academic article published since 1980.* This date may seem arbitrary, but we consider it a turning point because major citation systems shifted in the 1980s from numbered annotations to alphabetically ordered lists of references or works cited. As you read the article you select, you will, in four distinct but complementary ways, focus on a different dimension of the source's web of meaning, one at a time. Worknets typically pair a visual model and a written account that discusses the elements featured in the visual model. For the guiding examples that follow, we have developed visual diagrams using Dana Driscoll's "Introduction to Primary Research: Observations, Surveys, and Interviews," published in 2011. Driscoll explains in her article the differences between primary and secondary research, details types of qualitative research methods, and provides student examples of research projects to help readers conceptualize her advice about conducting primary research. Because her article ties so closely to what this book is about—research methods—we've selected it as a central source to model the worknets process.

Phase 1: Semantic Worknet— What Do Words Mean?

When creating a semantic worknet (Figure 3.1), you pay attention to words and phrases that are repeated throughout the central source ("semantics" is the study of meaning in words). Because academic writers repeat and return to concepts that they want readers to remember, by repetition we begin to understand the idea of a **keyword** or **keyphrase***—those words and phrases that are doing the work of advancing a source's central ideas. By noticing these key words and phrases, we understand first where they come from and how they have been initiated and second how they are being used to create a common

Keywords are increasingly important as part of knowledge-making. In published academic articles, keywords are tracked and collected so that we can easily find them through online database searches, telling us what central idea an article is forwarding.

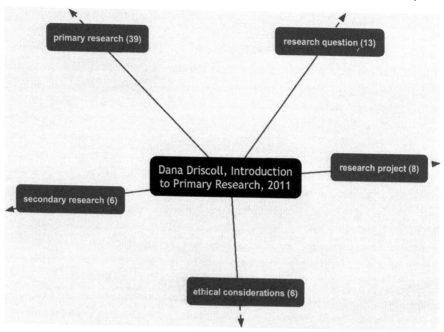

Figure 3.1. A semantic worknet. A center node identifies the article author and brief title. Five radiating nodes show frequently used two-word phrases, followed in parentheses by the number of times the phrase appeared: primary research (39), research question (13), research project (8), ethical considerations (6), and secondary research (6).

understanding between members of a particular academic discipline, community, or group of specialists. Although such keywords and phrases can at first seem inaccessible, strange, or confusing, noticing them and investigating their meaning is a sure way to begin grasping what the article is about, what knowledge it advances, and the audiences and purposes it aspires to reach.

There are several different ways to come up with a list of keywords and phrases. One approach is to manually circle or underline words and phrases as you read, noting them as they appear and re-appear in the text so you can return to them later. Other approaches make use of free online tools, such as TagCrowd (tagcrowd.com/), where you can copy and paste the text of the article and initiate a computer-assisted process that will yield a **concordance**, or a list of words and the number of times they appear in the text. NGram Analyzer (guidetodatamining.com/ngramAnalyzer/) is another effective tool for processing a text into a list of its one-, two-, and three-word phrases. Across multiple sources, beginning to find words and phrases that match up will help you locate key concepts for the literature review section of your research project.

A semantic worknet also helps you understand specialized vocabulary on your own terms, acting as a gateway into the terminology in the article. Noticing these words and phrases is a first step toward learning what the words and phrases mean. In Figure 3.1, you will see arrows extending outward from each term, radiating toward the edge of the image. This minor detail is a crucial feature of the worknet. It says that there is more, a deeper expanse beyond this article. That is, it suggests the generative reach of the words and phrases stemming from the article. Clearly an echo of the title, the phrase "primary research" appears in Driscoll's article 39 times, three times more than the next phrase, "research question," at 13. The article differentiates primary and secondary research. These keywords and phrases remind us of this. But the article also repeats the phrase "research project"

Try This: Finding Keywords (30 minutes)

You've chosen an article you consider to be interesting and relevant to your emerging research question. In anticipation of developing the semantic phase, spend time analyzing the article by doing the following:

- Read through the article, noting the title and any headings. Make a list of words that you find central to the text.

- Does the article provide a list of keywords at the beginning? If so, do any of them surprise you or differ from what you would have selected? Which ones overlap with the ones you compiled during your reading?

- Choose some of the keywords you've identified from the list supplied by the article or from the list you have generated. Next, without looking up any of the terms in the article or in any dictionary, attempt to write brief definitions of these terms. What does each keyword mean? Note with a star those terms you believe to be highly specialized.

and "ethical considerations." Each of these repeated keywords and phrases are included in the worknet.

After creating your worknet, we encourage you to create a 300–500 word written accompaniment of the visual worknet, based on the questions in the next "Try This," that helps you think through the "why" of the source's keywords and phrases. The notes you take as a part of the semantic worknet will not only give you a greater understanding of the central source you've read, but will also link to others in the conversation, giving you a fuller body of sources from which to orient your research proposal or project.

In addition to providing insight into the article, the family of ideas it advances, and the disciplinary orientation of the inquiry, noticing keywords and phrases can also inform further research, providing search terms relevant for exploring and locating related sources. It can lead you toward examining why an article covers some things with more repetition (in Driscoll's example, ethics), but not others (for example, finances and how they relate to ethical choices). When gaps appear between what a source says and does not say, those gaps are interesting places to orient your own research question.

Try This: Developing your Semantic Worknet (1–2 hours)

Select three to five keywords and develop the visual model demonstrated in Figure 3.1. After adding the appropriate nodes to the diagram, in 300-500 words, develop a critical reflection on your selected visual semantic worknet, using the following questions to guide you:

- What does each word or phrase mean, generally? What do they mean in the context of this specific article?

- Does the author provide definitions of the terms? More than one definition for each term? Are there examples in the article that illustrate more richly what the words or phrases do, how they work, or what they look like?

- Who uses these phrases, other than the author? For example, who are the people in the world who already know what "primary research" refers to? What kind of work do they do? Why?

Phase 2: Bibliographic Worknet—How do Sources Intersect and Draw from Each Other?

In the second phase of working with your central article, we ask you to investigate its **bibliography***—the list of sources that the author of your article has paraphrased, quoted, and summarized—by selecting, finding, and skimming or reading sources from the bibliography. (Bibliographies are located at the end of research articles; they may be titled "Works Cited," "References," or "Bibliography," depending on the documentation style.) You can choose any source that is found in the back matter, footnotes, or endnotes of your focal article to work with, and we recommend beginning with five or so. You might select the most significant sources—the ones that the author cited most frequently or drew from extensively—or you might simply select the ones that are most interesting to you. Either approach will be useful—they'll just yield different results. Attention to a source's *bibliography* is a way to begin tracing how sources use other sources to make their arguments. When we pay close attention to bibliographic references, we begin to see the links we might make 1) between keywords and phrases and a bibliography or Works Cited page and 2) between a central author and the sources with which they work. We begin to see that ideas don't just happen—they are connected to ideas that came before them. This foregrounds the interconnection of the article's main ideas and sources it draws upon, shedding light on the many ways in which academic research builds upon precedents by extending, challenging, and re-engaging historical texts.

Developing a bibliographic worknet like the one in Figure 3.2 calls attention to choices the author has made to invoke specific writers and researchers and their work in the article. It tells of a deeper and thicker entanglement, a web whose filaments extend beyond the obvious references into work that has gone before, sometimes recently, sometimes long before. By involving sources in the article, the author orients what are oftentimes central ideas while also associating those ideas (via the sources) with tangible, identifiable, and (sometimes) accessible precedents. This step is like the development of an annotated bibliography, or a list of sources relevant to a research project that include brief notes about the significance of a source to a wider conversation. An annotated

To notice a source in a bibliography and then to retrieve it and to read it can bloom into a research trajectory before unforeseen.

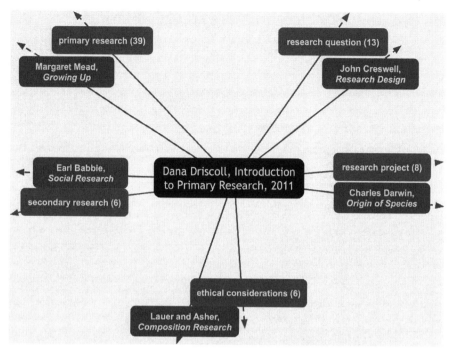

Figure 3.2. A bibliographic worknet added to Figure 3.1, the semantic
worknet. The center node continues to refer to the article author and
brief title. Five radiating nodes show short-form references to a small
sample of sources cited in the article: Earl Babbie, Social Research; John
Creswell, Research Design; Charles Darwin, Origin of Species; Lauer and
Asher, Composition Research; and Margaret Mead, Growing Up.

bibliography provides an invaluable intermediate step toward developing a literature review.

In a journal article, the sources an author cites are listed at the end of the
article. Their position implies secondary relevance. And yet the references
list is an invaluable resource for further tracing and for discovering, by following specific references back into the article, just how unevenly the sources
become involved in the article. That is, a references list makes sources appear
flat and equal, but among the sources listed, it is common to find that only a

quarter of them (or even less, sometimes) figure in substantial and sustained ways throughout the article. Many others are light, passing gestures. The bibliographic worknet can help you differentiate between the two and begin to notice which sources loom large and which are but briefly invoked.

Reading along and across the sources cited is akin to following leads and accepting invitations to further inquiry, formulating new or more nuanced research questions, and discovering influences that are intertwined, eclectic, and complementary. Finding a source and reading it alongside your focus article, too, can yield insights into the highly specific and situated ways writers use sources. For example, if you're researching climate change and just read a paraphrase or a brief quote from the National Oceanic and Atmospheric Administration at the Mauna Loa Observatory's 1958 data, you'll only have a part of the story. However, if you find that data and read it yourself, you might find that there are different parts of the data that you think are important to highlight. You might have a different perspective on the research, or you might find that you better understand the original article that led you to this text.

Try This: Developing Your Bibliographic Worknet (1–2 hours)

After adding the appropriate nodes to your diagram (as in Figure 3.2), in 300-500 words, develop a critical reflection on your selected visual bibliographic worknet, using the following questions to guide you:

- Which of these sources are available in the library? Which are available online?
- What is the average age of the sources? What might the date of the sources say about the timeliness of the article? What is the oldest source? Which is most recent?
- Are there sources that are inaccessible or out of circulation? How did the author locate such sources in the first place?
- How did the focus article use or incorporate the source materials? Were they glossed or briefly mentioned? Were large parts summarized into thin paraphrases? Were the whole of the works mentioned or just key ideas?
- Which of the sources, judging by its title, is most likely to cite other sources in the list? Which is least likely?

Try This: Developing a Rapid Prototype (30 minutes)

Before we go farther, let's pause and try this out. Notice that the first two phases of developing a worknet are concerned with things you will find in the source—keywords and phrases and sources cited. Work with any text you choose (an assigned reading for this class or another class or a source you can access quickly) to develop a **rapid prototype**, a swiftly hand-sketched radial diagram focusing only on the first two phases. You could share the diagram with someone who has read the same source and compare your radiating terms and citations. You could write about one or two of the terms or citations to anticipate their relevance to your emerging project. Or you could write about (or discuss) what the presence or absence of selected terms or sources says about the source you've chosen.

And/Or, Try This: Investigating Lists of Sources (1 hour)

Works cited or references lists may appear to be simple and flat add-ons at the end of an article or book, but we regard them to be rich resources for thinking carefully about a writer's choices. Look again at the works cited or references list for your chosen article, this time with an interest in coding and sorting it. This means you will look at the references list with the following questions to guide you:

- How recent are the sources in the list? Plot them onto a timeline to indicate the year of publication from oldest to newest. Which decade do most of the resources come from?
- How many of the sources are single-authored? How many are co-authored? How many are authored by organizations, companies, or other non-human entities (i.e., not by named human authors)?
- How many of the sources come from books? How many from journals? How many are available only online? How many are published open access?
- Ethical citation practices include awareness of the kind of voices represented through the works you've consulted. Given that you can only know so much about an author through a quick google search, consider what voices are included. Which voices are amplified, and which are missing altogether? You might consider developing a coding pattern to highlight the ways in which the authors represented identify in regard to gender, race, and ethnicity. Such an effort is fraught, yet it can begin to highlight patterns important for readers of sources to understand who is and is not being cited.

Among these patterns, which are significant for understanding the article, its authorship, or the contexts from which it was developed? What can you tell about the discipline or about the citation system based on coding the works cited or references list as you have?

Either way, your understanding of the original article, the larger research area, and the intersection between the two sources will deepen.

To create a bibliographic worknet, begin by reading the references list, footnotes, and endnotes and highlighting the sources that pique your curiosity. Once you've sampled from the list, take your sources to your library database to see what you can find. Try to locate three to five other sources from the bibliography, noting to yourself how difficult or easy these sources were to find. Once you've located your bibliographic sources, take a look at the pages that your central source cited and how the ideas on those pages were used in the focal source. Put the borrowed idea in context and try to figure out how and why your central source chose the bibliographic source to work with. Sampling from a bibliography, whether purposeful or random, can lead to promising new questions and promising new sources that can inform, guide, and shape your research questions. When you compose a 300–500 word written accompaniment of the bibliographic worknet, it is in service to thinking through where sources come from, how history marks sourcework, how findable sources really are, and how authors use other sources to create their key arguments.*

By the time you've collected three to five sources for your bibliographic worknet and noted some emergent key terms from your semantic worknet, you will be in good shape to begin to chart the major ideas, patterns, and distinctions among a group of sources. This will help you determine which sources hang together with a kind of "idea glue" that may help you, as a researcher, figure out which sources best frame your research question and which sources are less important in framing your research direction—this is how literature reviews begin to develop.

Believe it or not, a references list is a gift from an author to a reader and an invitation to follow paths of inquiry that are already well begun and often many years in motion.

Phase 3: Affinity Worknet—How Are Writers Connected?

In the third worknet phase, you pay attention to ties, connections, and relationships—affinities—between the central article's author and others in the research field you are exploring. An affinity worknet takes into account where

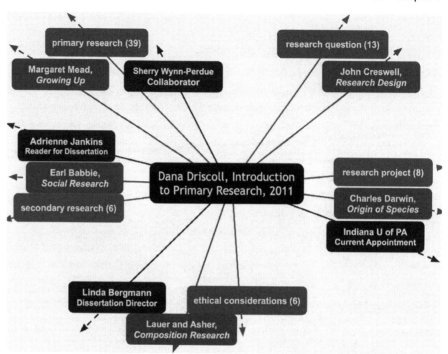

Figure 3.3. An affinity worknet (third phase), added to Figures 3.1 and 3.2. In this phase, four new nodes extend from the center, reflecting ties, connections, and relationships to the author: Adrienne Jankins, Reader for Dissertation; Linda Bergmann, Dissertation Director; Indiana U of PA, Current Appointment; and Sherry Wynn-Perdue, Collaborator.

the author has worked, what sorts of other projects she has taken up, and whom she has learned from, worked alongside, mentored, and taught. Many other authors are continuing research related to the article you have read. They are also keeping the company of people who do related work, whose research may complement or add perspective to the issues addressed in the article. You can see these relationships illustrated in the affinity worknet for our sample article in Figure 3.3.

As distinct from the first (semantic) and second (bibliographic) phases, the affinity worknet moves beyond the text and citations in the article; it is informed by activity and relationships in the world that may not be evident in the article itself. It begins to explore insights into an author's career and the interests that have shaped it. The focal article, for example, may bear close resemblance to other projects the author has worked on. Or her professional experience may suggest interplay among work history, current workplace responsibilities, and intellectual curiosities. Further, the people authors learn from and mentor are interconnected, participating in what is sometimes called an **invisible college**,* or a network of relations that operate powerfully and with varying degrees of formality and that influence the behind-the-scenes ways knowledge circulates throughout and across academic disciplines. The affinity worknet traces provisionally some of the shape of the collectives that have been a part of the author's work life. When you trace these relationships, you'll find that you have a much larger pile of sources to work from and directions for your work to follow—research centers, university programs, online forums, conference presentations, and multi-authored collaborations. As you compose a 300–500 word written record of the affinity worknet, you'll get a sense that academic writers don't emerge suddenly from isolation to compose rigorous work. Instead, they—like you—are real people, with real friends, colleagues, institutions, and collaborative relationships that sustain them. All of those relationships are also places that you might look to in order to orient your research project, as they offer you a glimpse into where your thinking comes from, how it is sustained, and where it gathers in space.

*For example, if you research the three authors of this text, you'll find that they have all co-authored other projects together, worked at the same institutions at times, and collaborated on research presentations.

Try This Together: Where Can I Find Affinities? (30 minutes)

Among the central premises in the affinity phase is that we can learn something about a writing researcher by noticing the company they keep. That is, by looking into professional and social relationships that have operated in their lives, we can begin to understand the larger systems of which their ideas—and their research commitments—are a part.

To treat this as its own research question would be to ask the following: What kinds of relationships can we learn about and by what means can we learn about them? Certainly simple Google searches may provide a start, but where else might you look? Work with a partner to generate a list of possible leads—platforms or social media venues where you might check to find out more about the lead author of the article you've chosen to work with.

Where can you find information about an author's affinities? A Google search for the author's name may lead you to an updated and readily available curriculum vitae, which is like an academic resume. Such a search might also lead to the author's social media activity (Facebook or Twitter accounts) or to a professional web site that provides additional details about collaborations and relationships. For perspective on intellectual genealogy related to a doctoral dissertation, you can turn to your library's database resources page and look into ProQuest Dissertations & Theses Global, which indexes information about major graduate projects and the people who participated on related committees. This lead can yield insight not only into who the author is and how she is connected to others but also into where an author's work comes from in the earliest stages of her career. You'll finish the affinity worknet having both a larger repertoire of research strategies and a wealth of people and places to lead you to other sources that you might not have otherwise thought of.*

Finding these affinities will also help you hone your research skills, allowing you to see that lives and connections can be traced through sources other than traditional library databases.

In fact, if you consider their overlapping affinity networks, you might more easily understand how this book came to be, how their collaborations and individual projects over the last decade or so coalesce in an interest in research methods and, in particular, explicit discussion of such methods with undergraduate students.

Try This: Writing about Your Affinity Worknet (1–2 hours)

After adding the appropriate nodes to the diagram (as in Figure 3.3), in 300-500 words, develop a critical reflection on your selected visual affinity worknet, using the following questions to guide you:

- What other kinds of work has this author written? When? For what audiences and purposes?
- Does the article in question bear resemblance to their other research? Does it seem to inform or influence their teaching or other responsibilities?
- Who has the author collaborated with on articles or on grants? What are the research interests and primary disciplines of these collaborators?
- Does the author appear to be active in online conversations? Where, and what do these interactions appear focused on? Are they professional and research-related or more casual and social?
- Where did the author study? With whom? What might be some of the ways these places and people influenced the author?

Phase 4: Choric Worknet—How Is Research Rhetorically Situated in the World?

With the fourth phase, worknets grow curioser, adding to the mix what we identify as choric elements. Choric elements take into account the time and place in which the article was produced. Choric worknets gather references to popular culture, world news, or the peculiarities and happenings that coincided with the article's being published. The term choric comes from the Greek, **khôra**, the wild, open surrounds as yet-unmapped and outside the town's street grid and infrastructure. Notice, too, the word's associations with chorus, or surrounding voices. With this in mind, we regard the choric worknet as exploratory and playful, engaging at the edges so that readers might wander just a bit. Sometimes our best ideas are those that seem, at first glance, to be farfetched.

Compared to the other phases, the choric worknet orbits in wider and weirder circles, drifting into uncharted and therefore potentially inventive linkages. Considering the time and place in which an article was written helps bring us as readers to that time and place. Venturing into the coincidental surrounds can lead to eureka moments, inspiring clicks of insight, curiosity, and possibility, but it can also prove to be too far flung, too peculiar to be useful. This is one of the lessons of research: sometimes we spend time on what we think will be useful, but as any Googler-down-the-rabbit-hole-of-YouTube knows, sometimes what we think will be useful isn't. Yet it is in the trying that we learn how to weed out as well as how to hold close what is exciting, original, and odd.

This phase encourages you to find those rabbit holes, if only for a moment. Begin with the year your focal article was published, where the author wrote it, and begin an online search, paying attention to what was happening in the world that year. Follow your hunches, your interests, and even the ways that what you've found in the other worknet phases maps on to where your meandering is going. Look at Figure 3.4 and you will see five choric nodes. Their selection came from 30 minutes of online searches related to 2011, primarily, and also a few related to Southeast Michigan, Detroit, and Oakland University, the university where Dana Driscoll worked when she wrote the

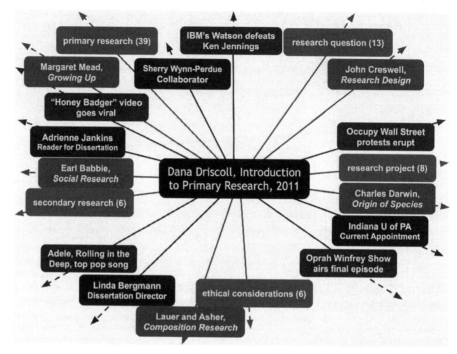

Figure 3.4. A choric worknet (fourth phase), added to Figure 3.3. The center node continues to refer to the article author and brief title. Five radiating nodes refer to events that happened in 2011: "Honey Badger" video goes viral, IBM's Watson defeats Ken Jennings, Occupy Wall Street protests erupt, Oprah Winfrey Show airs final episode, and Adele's "Rolling in the Deep" was the top pop song.

article. Each of the five nodes reflects your choice, something note-worthy or intriguing.

The choices you make in creating the nodes can spark the beginnings of researchable questions and may be reflected in your 300–500 word account of the choric worknet. For example, the node for the "Honey Badger" video going viral as it coincides with Driscoll's article on primary research methods might instigate research questions concerning just what kind of researched claims the video makes, the relationship of video to writing, and the edge of seriousness and playfulness in composing research that will circulate publicly. This element in the choric worknet, although it at first may seem trivial, can also pique curiosity and invite inquiries into what animals know or into their biology and ecology, such as in the *This American Life* podcast episode, "Becoming a Badger." For any student who began reading their focal article with few ideas about their own research path, the choric phase will give you an abundance of options to test and play with the limits and openings of a research project.

Given the messiness of invention—its combinations of purpose and digression, insight and failure, getting lost and then deciding on a direction—the choric worknet stands as the most wide open, potentially the richest of the four phases, even as it risks being the most wasteful, inviting oddball and offbeat ties. Such ties, however, situate the article in the wider world, and they do so while also honoring the place you stand as a researcher, tapping into the interests and curiosities that compel you most.

Try This: Writing about Your Choric Worknet (1–2 hours)

After adding the appropriate nodes to the diagram, in 300-500 words, develop a critical reflection on your selected visual choric worknet, using the following questions to guide you:

- What was happening in the wider world coincident with the time and place of the focal article's being written and published?
- Why have you selected the assortment of nodes you have? How did you find them? What about them compelled you to add them to the worknet?
- Where do you locate possibilities for further exploration and for emerging interests at the juncture of any choric node and any other node in the radial diagram?
- Which of the choric nodes is most relevant, in your view? Which is least?
- Are there choric nodes you thought about including but later abandoned? What motivated you to make such choices?

Branching Out—Taking Worknets Farther

With the four phases completed, as in Figure 3.5, the worknet introduces initial, inventive branchings, a web of filaments, or trails, that invite further inquiry and that may prime further questions. When experienced researchers read scholarly sources, they usually do so to support, reinforce, or clarify claims they have already begun to formulate. In early stages of research, however, reading scholarly sources oftentimes yields more questions, and these questions each set up further inquiry. Worknets position scholarly sources as resources for invention, and after

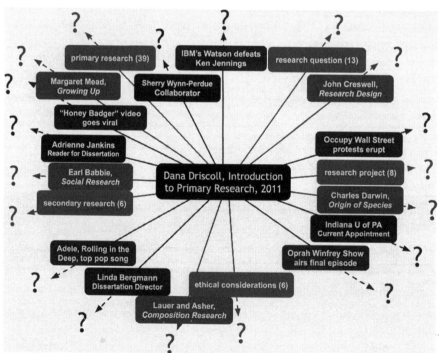

Figure 3.5. A finalized four-phase worknet. The worknet primes yet more questions from each peripheral node. Each node may prompt associations that motivate database searches, online lookups, or ideas for promising new directions.

developing all four phases, you will begin to see that you have many more options for expanding your emerging interests than you initially realized. This approach resonates with the idea of **copia**,* or lists of possibilities, which suggests that having more than you need to continue research is a wonderful place to be.

While a single worknet can engage us with new ideas entangled in a web of relationships extending from an article, a series of worknets—that is, worknets applied to two or three or more related articles—can form the foundation for a substantial backdrop to a research project. In fact, a compilation of worknets provides you with the basis of a literature review, that portion of a researched project that provides orientation to established research related to your area of inquiry.

When we write with copious questions—just as worknets provide—we rarely run out of things to say. Allowing for this wandering helps us think more abundantly about what there is to say on a topic, what is still unknown, and how we can follow the research paths that most ignite our passions.

■ Really Getting to Know Your Sources

Worknets provide a stepwise process to get to know your sources. The better known and better read the sources, the more nuanced and precise will be the literature review that emerges from your work with them. Certainly there are other intermediate note-keeping options and less involved approaches to the phases presented in this chapter. For example, an annotated bibliography might require you to gather and write brief summaries of related sources, focusing on the relevance of the source to your research question. Whether you take up the method we introduce and produce a full, complete worknet for one source, or whether you apply selections of the phases to one or more articles, perhaps adapting by writing annotations or sketching worknets by hand, the approach introduced here will help shape your own work.

Try This: Finding Connections, Near and Far (30 minutes)

The choric nodes are the most likely to introduce variety and surprise. They fan out the article's web of relations, finding (possible) connections that may hint at new or slightly altered researchable questions. After you develop the choric phase of the worknet for your chosen article, identify both the node you consider to be *most related* and the node you consider to be *least related*. Write for five minutes on each node, accounting for why you think it to be more or less related. What do each of these nodes indicate about the world from which the article emerged? What do each of these nodes say about what you find interesting or about your own curiosities in this context?

■ Modeling Worknets

We have seen students do distinctive, innovative work with worknets, and we're spotlighting one such example to give you an idea of what is possible. One undergraduate student at Virginia Tech applied all four phases to a 2015 article by Armond Towns, "That Camera Won't Save You! The Spectacular Consumption of Police Violence." The article discusses issues related to body cameras, social justice, police violence, and the presumed security bestowed on technological devices. In this case, the worknet followed the steps introduced in this article, culminating in all four phases layered into Figure 3.6.

Additionally, the student was invited to translate the visual and textual worknet into a 3D model, using materials from a local art supply store. The model materialized the worknet as a physical sculpture, conveying more fully an understanding of the article as entangled with the words, sources, relation-

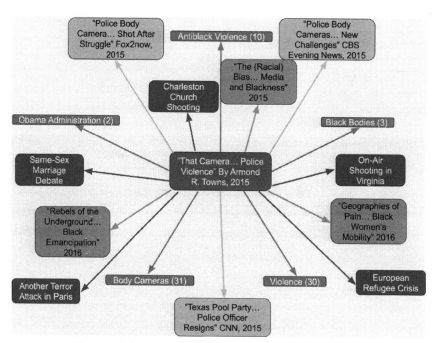

Figure 3.6. A sample worknet created by Alonda Johnson.

ships, and time-place coincidences of the moment in which it was produced. Figure 3.7 shows the potential of extending the worknet one step farther by creating a model whose dimensions and materials exceed the page or the screen.

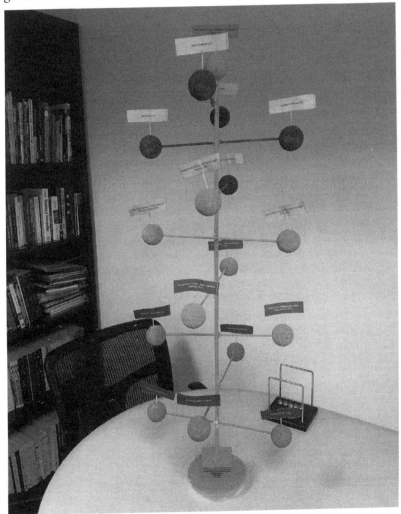

Figure 3.7. A three-dimensional, material model of the sample worknet created by Alonda Johnson.

Using Worknets to Develop a Literature Review

Although literature reviews serve different purposes from discipline to discipline and vary in scope from one project to another, they have in common the purpose of orienting readers to relevant scholarship. Literature reviews provide a synthesis, or glancing overview, that weaves together relevant focuses and acknowledges limitations, or knowledge gaps, in the series of sources gathered in the review. By the time you've finalized a worknet, you will have read and skimmed at least ten sources around a common research theme and question that interests you. Looking again, consider some of the ways specific worknet phases can support your development of a literature review:

- **Semantic worknet** (phase 1): How are specific keywords and phrases used differently from one source to another? How do different keywords and phrases across a selection of sources suggest yet more refined possibilities for impactful terms not yet introduced in the sources gathered?

- **Bibliographic worknet** (phase 2): How do the articles you have collected respond to common sources? What can be said about each article's timeliness based on the ages of the sources it consults?

- **Affinity worknet** (phase 3): How do connections with other people or institutions reveal the priorities of the authors of your sources? What can you discern about the relationship of each article to an academic discipline?

- **Choric worknet** (phase 4): What is the relationship of each article to contemporary events? How might those events have influenced its message?

With a series of worknets built from different but related sources, you have carried out a generative, robust method for assembling, annotating, and interweaving sources. Literature reviews require thoughtful balancing of sources, making reference to sources so they are represented concisely and fairly. Worknets, for the practice they give you with moving in and out of texts, support the development of effective literature reviews.

Focus on Delivery: Writing a Literature Review

A literature review is a synthesized grouping of academic sources that have been chosen to frame a larger piece of research and that relate to a research question a writer is pursuing. Some literature reviews are stand-alone pieces to say "this is what's out there on a particular topic." Most literature reviews are front matter for larger academic papers. The scope of your project will determine how many sources go into your literature review.

By "literature," we mean academic scholarship chosen about a certain topic that helps to answer a particular research question. By "review," we mean a summary of the literature's argument and an explanation of its connection to the other sources that you use.

To write a literature review, complete these steps:

1. Locate five to ten sources that you think would be useful for understanding the research question.

2. Skim these sources.

3. If the source is relevant to your research question, read it fully and *annotate* it, writing a 100-word summary of the source in your own words. Read the source's bibliography to add relevant sources you find there to your working source list.

4. Discard irrelevant sources and locate ones that are more specific to your research question. Annotate all relevant sources.

5. Read your 100-word summaries and try to figure out how they go together. What are their common features, key words, and theoretical frameworks? What year were they written? Could sources be grouped historically, theoretically, or thematically?

6. Use your worknets to help you group your sources in different ways in order to see patterns between and among your sources:

    a. What similar ideas and words are used to discuss major ideas in your research area among your sources? How do they differ? (semantic)

    b.   What changes when you move your sources into chronological order from earliest to latest or latest to most recent? (bibliographic)

    c.   What happens when you group sources by relationships between and among sources? (affinity)

    d.   Would your review benefit from adding historical and cultural context? (choric)

5.   Consider how these sources together lead up to your research question. Why is it important, timely, and relevant to previous research?

6.   Revise your annotations and put them together in such a way that the connections between them are clear and the connections to your research question are visible.

What's important for you to know about literature reviews is that the choices about what sources to use and what makes them go together are not immediately clear for a reader, which means part of writing a literature review is including that rationale within the review itself. By reading your literature review, your audience should be able to figure out the "idea glue" that holds all of the literature together, inclusive of your project's purpose and the main conversations taking place within your research area. A reader should walk away from your literature review knowing exactly why you've chosen these sources to go together, as opposed to millions of others that could be chosen instead.

■ Works Cited

Driscoll, Dana L. "Introduction to Primary Research: Observations, Surveys, and Interviews." *Writing Spaces: Readings on Writing,* edited by C. Lowe and P. Zemliansky, vol. 2, WritingSpaces.org/Parlor Press/The WAC Clearinghouse, 2011, pp. 153–74. The WAC Clearinghouse, wac.colostate.edu/docs/books/writingspaces2/driscoll—introduction-to-primary-research.pdf.

Glass, Ira, host. "Becoming a Badger." *This American Life,* episode 596, WBEZ, 9 Sept. 2016, www.thisamericanlife.org/596/becoming-a-badger.

Johnson, Alonda. "3D Model of Worknet for Armond Towns' 'That Camera Won't Save You! The Spectacular Consumption of Police Violence.'" 14 Nov. 2018.

ENGL1105: First-year Writing: Introduction to College Composition, Virginia Polytechnic Institute and State University, student work.

Johnson, Alonda. "Worknet of Armond Towns' 'That Camera Won't Save You! The Spectacular Consumption of Police Violence.'" 14 Nov. 2018. ENGL1105: First-year Writing: Introduction to College Composition, Virginia Polytechnic Institute and State University, student work.

Towns, Armond R. "That Camera Won't Save You! The Spectacular Consumption of Police Violence." *Present Tense: A Journal of Rhetoric in Society*, vol. 5, no. 2, 2015, www.presenttensejournal.org/volume-5/that-camera-wont-save-you-the -spectacular-consumption-of-police-violence/.

"Trends in Atmospheric Carbon Dioxide." *Carbon Cycle Greenhouse Gases, NOAA Global Monitoring Laboratory,* 5 Oct. 2021, gml.noaa.gov/ccgg/trends/.

Chapter 4. Working With Words

Writing is a technology. Writing allows us to capture otherwise ephemeral conversations and ideas, to put words down on paper. Current concerns about technology echo the original complaints (circa fifth century BCE) about writing: it makes it easier for others to cheat, it hurts our in-person relationships, it's not trustworthy, and it's making us stupid. Despite these concerns (and it's worth analyzing these concerns to consider where they come from and whether or not they're fair), many of our most popular technologies continue to change in ways that make it easier to access and capture words. For one, the computer developed as a counting machine, which has morphed into a tool that, among many things, allows us to consume words to our hearts' content. Although the telephone originally allowed us to speak to each other directly, plenty of people never speak on their phones anymore—they just send written messages. All of this to say: we love words, and we have access to copious amounts of them.

Digital technologies have been a boon for researchers, since we now have so many tools that help us find, sort, count, and analyze word patterns in discursive **corpuses**,* or groupings of compositions. Such treatment of words, in which we consider the relationship between a text and its social context, is broadly called **discourse analysis**, and in this chapter we will address one particular approach to discourse analysis that considers language in social interaction. In Chapter 3, you had the opportunity to practice word work by developing your semantic worknet. During this phase you used **content analysis**—counting words, noting their proximity to other words, and identifying key concepts in part by their frequency and placement in the text. Another way to understand the relationships between words and social context is to conduct **rhetorical analysis**, keying in on the rhetorical situation in which a particular composition develops. Finally, **genre analysis** considers how the particular kind of text you are examining functions like a cultural artifact, providing clues about the context in which it developed.

All of these methods—discourse analysis, content analysis, rhetorical analysis, and genre analysis—are ways of examining words and the detailed sto-

> Corpus is Latin for "body" (as in body of work or body of information), which has the same root as corpse—a totally different kind of body.

ries they tell about social interaction and rhetorical contexts. These analytical methods demonstrate the significance of word patterns we are able to observe in texts all around us. Charles Antaki, Michael Billig, Derek Edwards, and Jonathan Potter have worked together to suggest that the key to success in such analyses is actually *doing analysis*. This may seem rather common sense, but analysis is probably the hardest part of conducting effective research. By insisting that doing analysis means *doing analysis,* Antaki and his co-authors mean that analytical tools are not equations in which you can simply plug in a few variables and unlock a fixed meaning. They note that analysis is not

- simply pointing out the weaknesses in someone else's work,
- just sharing findings,
- summarizing the research, or
- stating an opinion.

Instead, analysis

- is a messy process,
- connects findings within a larger rhetorical context,
- describes significance of emergent patterns, and
- explains the "so what" component of the work to an audience.

Analysis helps us understand not just what words say but also what they *do*, not just what they represent but also how they *mean*. Analysis is a foundational activity for successful, effective research writing, and it is also the starting place for production, design, and delivery—processes that we will address in subsequent chapters. Delivery, in particular, is often the concern with which people start—how will I write up my research? What will it look like? What words will I use? But we encourage you to be patient. Effective research takes time, and it can/should be messy along the way. You can't know what you'll write until you have asked and answered your research question by wholly engaging in the analysis, getting pulled into the analysis, getting lost in the analysis! And then—when you've identified the significance of your findings—turn to Chapter 8 and consider methods for writing up your research.

■ Discourse Analysis

Discourse analysis is a qualitative research method, and the many varieties of discourse analysis constitute the area of research called discourse studies, which are practiced in social science and humanities disciplines. For our purposes we will focus on discourse analysis (DA) that examines language in social interaction, which includes language communicated through talk, text, and gesture. Since our focus in this chapter is on words, we will walk through the following steps:

1. Considering how you select a discursive corpus, a group of texts for analysis;
2. Exploring and identifying the **rhetorical situation**, or the context in which communication takes place, for the corpus; and
3. Preparing or **transcribing** discourse, that is, moving from discourse in interaction—the kind of talk that might happen with a friend during the day, in an interview setting, or on a digital platform—to written words on a page.

After you've selected a corpus, explored its development, identified its rhetorical situation, and prepared it for analysis, then the fun really begins: tagging or coding patterns in the text and interpreting findings. We'll save these last two steps for the end of the chapter when we'll ask you to develop a coding scheme for the corpus and method of analysis that you select.

■ Identifying a Corpus

There are lots of starting places for word work. You might already have a research question, so you might need to identify the corresponding corpus that will help you answer your question. Or, you might stumble upon an interesting text or idea, and though you may have questions, your thoughts may not have crystalized into clear research questions as yet. Wherever you are in the process, you will have to identify a set of meaningful words, the data that will help you answer a research question. Some examples of corpuses include the following:

- **Conversation as corpus:** Discourse analyst Dorothy Smith chronicles transcribed accounts of the friends of a woman—simply referred to as "K"—who support the suggestion that she is mentally ill. Smith critiques both the friends' accounts and the line of questioning that the interviewer provides, suggesting that together they develop an idea of "K" as mentally ill, though the facts do not necessarily support their finding. Smith uses her analysis to demonstrate that interviews are co-constructed and that interviewers have significant power in the accounts they elicit.

- **Digital text as corpus:** Jennifer Gonzalez writes about education on her blog, Cult of Pedagogy. She has lots of articles posted, but some are much more popular than others, and some stir controversy. Responsiveness to her posts can be measured, in part, by the number of comments she receives on each post. A researcher could use the comments on her posts, her posts alone, or these texts together as a research corpus.

Narrowing a corpus to a specific time can help with establishing a well-defined scope (e.g., one hour of conversation, a Twitter hashtag across one week or one month, a print archive in a specific year).

- **Social media as corpus:** Recently, a student followed the Tennessee Titans' twitter feed for a month and used the entirety of their tweets as a corpus.* In her analysis, she was able to note how frequently the Titans tweeted, when and what they tweeted, how many times the team was retweeted or responded to, and discursive patterns in their tweets.

- **Print archive as corpus:** You may have a stack of texts in your home, library, or university that are ripe for analysis. Kate's university was recently gifted an incredible archive of 1500 letters written by schoolchildren to Holocaust survivor Nessy Marks. Her students began digitizing and cataloging this rich archive, learning about the schoolchildren's reactions to elements of Ms. Marks' story that range from admissions of family connections to the holocaust to demonstrations of patriotism.

- **"Homely Discourse" as corpus:** Carolyn Miller has suggested that "homely discourse" such as "the recommendation, the user manual, the progress report, the ransom note, the lecture, and the white paper, as well as the eulogy, the apologia, the inaugural, the public proceeding, and the sermon" are all worthy of analysis (155). In fact, "everyday" texts, such as greeting cards and menus, can be fascinating corpuses. Paige Lenssen published her study of Enron's "honest services clause," certainly homely discourse within the larger body of the company's corporate documents. Her work, published in the student journal *Xchanges*, traces the company's breaches of ethics before their collapse.

In Chapter 1 we defined research as the systematic asking of questions and congruent use of methods to learn answers to interesting, important questions. In selecting a corpus we once again encourage you to tap into your curiosities as a starting place for research.

Try This Together: Identifying Corpuses (30 minutes)

With a small group, follow your curiosities and select an example for each of the kinds of corpuses listed here:

- **Identify a conversation as corpus.** This could be a face-to-face conversation, a video, an audio recording, or a textual conversation.
- **Select a digital text that you might consider for analysis.** This might be a blog, journal manuscript, newspaper article, etc.
- **Choose a social media corpus.** This can come from any digital platform, but make sure to narrow your selection such that you choose a particular thread, post, hashtag, or set of comments. Oftentimes, social media researchers organize corpuses, or corpora, by following designated timeframes or hashtags.

Look for a print archive. This could be an extensive personal magazine collection, a trove of letters, or something within your university library's holdings.

- **Lastly, find some homely discourse.** Look around you and find some "everyday" texts that you might not have initially considered for analysis. These texts might be signs, posters, forms, advertisements, cards, or similar. Sometimes the more "homely" or unexpected, the more interesting the analysis!

As you search for these various corpuses, take particular note of how you find them, what draws you to them, and what further analysis of them might glean for you.

■ Exploring and Establishing the Context

Once you have identified an interesting corpus, harness your detective skills and spend some time exploring. Consider the playful approach to learning about a text that you developed in Chapter 3 when you constructed a worknet. Draw on that same willingness to experiment and follow leads down rabbit holes in your approach to learning about the corpus you have identified.

■ Taking Notes As You Go

Preparing your corpus for analysis is part of the research process, so make note of what you find as you go. This means annotate your corpus, note your experiences at every step along the research path, and consider these observations and annotations in your final analysis. An annotation is a short summary of work, whether a book or textual source (as in writing your literature review), or an observational experience (like a site visit or a response to data collection). There are lots of ways to annotate, and we encourage you to try different methods and combine them along the way until you find what works best for you.

Try This: Identify the Rhetorical Context of a Corpus (30 minutes)

Now that you have identified potential research spaces, return one more time to the corpus that you find most interesting to explore it and identify its rhetorical contexts. Consider the following:

- By whom and how were the texts in the corpus developed?
- For whom and why were the texts in the corpus developed?
- What is the context in which the texts in the corpus were developed?
- When were the texts in the corpus created?

Essentially, consider the *Who, What, When, Where, Why,* and *How* of these texts. Then, spend some time looking slant at the text, i.e., consider what surrounds the text—the other authors, texts, images, and contexts that impact its uptake.

Chapter 3*	Consider our discussion of the components of annotations.
Chapter 5	Think about the steps we suggest in composing a research memo.
Chapter 6	Peruse our recommendations about developing an annotated map.
Lists of questions	Take a page from writing teacher Michael Bunn, who encourages us to "Read Like Writers," asking questions of texts before, during, and after we read them.
Double-entry journal	On one side of the page make notes about your research experiences and specific steps in your process, and on the other side reflect on those experiences in subsequent considerations of your data.
Research log	Create a log to catalogue your responses to the text and your initial impressions - these will be helpful when you begin coding your corpus.
Study formal features	Consider the formal aspects of the text (how long is it? how is it structured? does it have headings or images?) as well as your thoughts, feelings, and analyses.

Note taking strategies often change from one research project to the next. We encourage you to try these approaches and to ask your classmates how they take notes.

Experiment with these different methods, and don't forget the material components of annotation. For instance, selecting a particular pen, paper, app, or digital format for creating your annotations can usefully change your approach to a corpus. You can record your observations and analyses on the text itself, in a separate document, in a journal, or using audio, video, or images. You might also combine some of these modes and create a multimodal response or annotation. There are some digital platforms that allow you to provide audio or image tags within corpora; such practice is a great way to start coding a selected corpus.

■ Preparing the Corpus for Analysis

You may have easy access to your selected corpus, and it may even be made of digital text that is easily manipulable. If so, awesome! However, if you're working with print text that you'll need to digitize to code more easily, or if you're working with an audio conversation that you'll need to transcribe, you may need to take some time to prepare the text for analysis. Be persistent if you need to take this step. Preparing text for analysis is an interpretive act, and it can be just as interesting as analysis. In fact, it may allow you a closeness to the data that might make things easier as you begin analysis.

If you are examining print texts, you may want to copy or scan your corpus and then preserve the originals. You may want to curate your archive (see the discussion of working with archives and curating collections in Chapter 6). Digitizing your corpus may be helpful, but it is not necessary. You may instead want to work with print versions of your texts. Either way, make sure that you can annotate and fully examine the corpus you've selected without damaging the original.

If you are working with a spoken or gestural conversation, you will need to transcribe the discourse. Transcription translates words from one mode to another, and you can decide what level of detail you need for the work you are doing. For instance, you may select a minimal level of detail for transcription that simply records what has been said in a conversation. However, you might want to capture much more—the way something has been phrased or extratextual sounds that make up a conversation, including laughter and sighs, emphasis, pauses, gestures, facial expressions. Analysts who practice a version of discourse analysis called conversation analysis believe that for analysis, you need all the components of a given conversation, so their transcription is very detailed, and it might be hard to read for someone who isn't familiar with the method.

Many discourse analysts who study language in social interaction employ an interim level of detail that includes text, pause, and emphasis. Figure 4.1 includes an extract of conversation between a writing consultant and a student in the Writing Center. The number that precedes each line allows the analyst to easily reference particular moments in the conversation for analysis. The capital letter with the colon following it indicates who is speaking, in this case the "G" indicates the student, and the "T" indicates the tutor. The bracket "[" indicates overlapping speech, and the parenthesis indicates a pause in the conversation "(.)". The conversation is aligned so that it's easy to read. Such an approach to transcription makes it accessible, and the audience has a fairly good idea of how the speech was delivered. The thing is, whatever you choose to transcribe should be something you address in analysis. So if you don't plan to analyze facial expression, there's no need to transcribe facial expression.

Extract 1

55	G:	You don't have to read it like (.) you can read it quietly. I mean,
56		I've got other stuff that I can do.
57	T:	Well maybe what we can do is actually (.) to make sure that your
58		meaning and intentions are clear. So maybe I'll read the first ten lines out
59		[loud
60	G:	[O.K.
61	T:	And we can make sure we're on the same um (.) paycheck.

Figure 4.1. Example of a transcribed conversation.

Try This: Transcribe a Video (60 minutes)

One of the most exciting parts of transcription is how it helps you really be attentive to words used in interaction. What we initially notice when we listen to or watch something is so different than what we notice upon second, third, or fourth attempts at listening/seeing. When we transform audio/gestural data to written data, this effect is compounded. Follow these steps to try transcription for yourself:

1. Select a brief video (30 seconds is ideal!) that includes interaction between at least two people.

2. Before you transcribe, watch/listen to the video at least three times. After each viewing, take notes about what stands out to you. How does your analysis gain detail with each subsequent viewing?

3. Now that you're becoming more familiar with the excerpt, after your third viewing, compile all your notes and transcribe this discourse, attempting to capture the multiple methods of communication (textual, gestural, oral) in words.

4. To effectively transcribe the interaction, you'll need to watch or listen to it many more times. Transcription is much easier if you can also slow down the video or audio. After you've completed the transcription at the end of your third viewing, take notes about what stands out to you after spending considerably more time with this text. How does this impression differ from the first three viewings and your notes about the experiences? What do these differences suggest about your relationship to the corpus, to time, and sense-making?

■ Content Analysis

We may be able to discern a text's focal concerns by noticing the words and phrases that repeat within it. Similarly, patterns of omission help researchers account for underrepresented, downplayed, or altogether ignored matters.

Content analysis is practiced in numerous fields; it is a systematic approach to examining patterns in data and provides a quantitative treatment of discourse. For instance, you might consider how many times a particular term, phrase, theme, or, more generally, **code**, is mentioned in a text and then analyze its significance to the document's purpose or context. Returning again to the semantic phase of the worknets detailed in Chapter 3, patterns surfaced through content analysis can be useful for understanding a text or corpus you're analyzing, and it can also be insightful when applied to your own writing. In both cases—applied to your own writing or to the writing of others—content analysis helps us develop an **indexical awareness**.* By indexical awareness, we mean that as writers or as readers, content analysis clarifies patterns of repetition and omission, or patterns of what is and is not there.

Try This: Content Analysis of a Text (60 minutes)

Use content analysis to examine your own text. Start by selecting something you have recently written. Then, copy the text into a document or use an app that allows you to quantify the corpus (word processing software can help you do this, as can free apps that develop word clouds and visualizations, like Voyant Tools (voyant-tools.org/), TagCrowd (tagcrowd.com/), NGram Analyzer (guidetodatamining.com/ngramAnalyzer/), and AntConc (www.laurenceanthony.net/software/antconc/), if you want to get advanced. Now, spend some time analyzing the corpus:

- Identify **word frequency**: What are the most frequently used words in the corpus? How many times are they mentioned?
- Identify **collocation**: Which words are located next to each other? How frequently are they located next to each other?
- Consider **uptake**: If you've shared this text with others, perhaps through social media, how many individuals have liked or shared it? What is the life of the thread? Does it change or switch platforms?
- Identify **textual patterns**: How many words are in each paragraph? In each sentence?

■ Rhetorical Analysis

Whereas discourse analysis examines patterns, often of language in interaction, and content analysis considers quantifiable, systemic patterns in discourse, rhetorical analysis considers the context, audience, and purpose for discourse. Rhetorical analysis helps demonstrate the significance of a text by carefully considering the rhetorical situation in which it develops and the ways that it supports its purpose. There are lots of definitions of rhetoric, and the definition that makes the most sense to you and your understanding of communication will impact how you deploy rhetorical analysis. Here are a few definitions of rhetoric:

The ancient Greek rhetor, **Aristotle**: "Rhetoric may be defined as the faculty of observing in any given case the available means of persuasion."

British rhetorician, **I. A. Richards**: "Rhetoric…should be a study of misunderstanding and its remedies" (3).

Contemporary American rhetors, **Elizabeth Wardle** and **Doug Downs**: "Rhetoric is a field of study in which people examine how persuasion and communication work, and it is also the art of human interaction, communication, and persuasion" (366).

Contemporary American genre theorist, **Charles Bazerman**: "The study of how people use language and other symbols to realize human goals and carry out human activities. . . . ultimately a practical study offering people greater control over their symbolic activity" (6).

Rhetorical analysis helps us understand the various components that make a communicative act/artifact successful or not. A key component to effective rhetorical analysis is careful, active attention to what the author and her text are trying to accomplish. Krista Ratcliffe calls such attention **rhetorical listening**.

Try This: Defining Rhetoric (30 minutes)

Find a few alternative definitions of rhetoric on your own, and see which one is most appealing to you. Now, mush them together, paraphrase, and come up with a definition that resonates with your understanding of rhetoric.

Most people summarize rhetorical listening as an orientation of active openness toward communication, and Ratcliffe identifies multiple components for such a stance:

- "acknowledging the existence" of the other, their self, and discourse
- "listening for (un)conscious presences, absences, and unknowns"
- purposefully "integrating this information into our world views and decision making" (29)

Rhetorical listening often draws our attention to absences. Jacqueline Jones Royster's work on literacy practices, particularly of nineteenth century Black women, demonstrates how listening for and being curious about absences often leads us to understudied rhetors. Temptaous McCoy has coined the term **amplification rhetorics (AR)**, a method of seeking out and amplifying rhetorical practices that may not have been effectively heard. She describes AR as a way of examining and celebrating the experiences and community rhetorics of Black and marginalized communities.

Try This: Analyzing Keywords (60 minutes)

Working with something you have recently written, assign keywords (one or two-word phrases) you believe would do well to convey its significance (don't count, just consider what you think is most important about the text). To do so, follow these steps:

1. Identify five to seven keywords based on your sense of the text.

2. Then, turn to a keyword generating tool, such as TagCrowd (tagcrowd.com) or the NGram Analyzer (guidetodatamining.com/ngramAnalyzer/). Copy and paste your writing into the platform and initiate the analysis with the aid of the keyword generating tool. Which words or phrases match (as in, you thought they were significant and they show up frequently in your text)? Which words or phrases appear in one list but not the other? What do you think explains the differences in the lists?

3. Next, identify two keywords or phrases you believe are not sufficiently represented in either list. What are these keywords or phrases, and how are they significant to the work you are doing? Develop a one-page revision memo that accounts for how you could go about expanding the presence of these underrepresented words or phrases in your writing.

Another way of thinking of rhetorical listening in the context of texts is Peter Elbow's practice of "The Believing Game," in which he encourages audience members to suspend potential disbelief or critique of a text. Instead of starting with critique, he works to step into the authors' shoes and actually believe whatever they are suggesting. Complimentary to this practice is Sonja K. Foss and Cindy L. Griffin's formulation of **invitational rhetoric**. They offer invitational rhetoric as counter to understandings of rhetoric as primarily about persuasion, like Aristotle's definition of rhetoric. They see persuasion as ultimately about power, whereas invitational rhetoric instead works to develop equitable relationships. Like rhetorical listening, invitational rhetoric is a method for establishing understanding within relationships. They define such work as "an invitation to the audience to enter the rhetor's world and see it as the rhetor does" (5). Although these approaches all differ, what they have in common is using rhetorical awareness to invite understanding rather than arguing for one's own point of view or "winning" an argument.

Try This: Rhetorical Analysis (60 minutes)

Practice rhetorical analysis. Select an article that interests you, perhaps one that you identified to work with in Chapter 3 or something you came across when you searched for potential corpora at the beginning of this chapter. Spend some time considering why this article is persuasive or appealing to you:

- **Who is the audience?** What evidence suggests this audience?
- **What is the context in which it was written?** What evidence suggests this?
- **What is its purpose?** You might also identify the thesis or orienting principle and consider the larger relationship between the work's purpose and its stated argument or principle. What evidence leads you to this finding?
- **Who is the author?** Really—who is the author? Draw on your worknet findings and consider the author's relationship to this rhetorical situation. What is the exigency, or reason, for writing this work?

Or, you might return to considering the *Who, What, When, Where, Why,* and *How* of this article.

There are many ways to practice rhetorical analysis, although it is often reduced to an equation rather than a tool for discovery of a text. Let rhetorical analysis be a method that opens up understanding and possibility rather than one that simply labels certain words or passages. Consider how identifying a particular rhetorical appeal adds depth and nuance to a text and connects you to it in complex ways. For instance, the previous "Try This" offered two approaches to rhetorical analysis. The next "Try This" offers two additional approaches. Consider which one resonates most with you. Which method helps you identify the significance and interest of a text?

Try This: More Rhetorical Analysis (60 minutes)

Working with a text/genre/corpus of your choosing, develop responses to the following prompt. If you seek a text as the basis of your analysis, we recommend Captain Brett Crozier's letter to shipmates aboard the aircraft carrier Theodore Roosevelt during the 2020 COVID-19 outbreak, which was published by the San Francisco Chronicle (s3.documentcloud.org/documents/6939308/TR-COVID-19-Assistance-Request.pdf).

In what ways does the author offer specific appeals to the audience? Consider particular instances of the following appeals in the text:

- **Kairos**, which refers to timeliness—indications of why the text is contemporarily relevant
- **Ethos**, which we addressed in detail in Chapter 2, generally concerns the relative credibility of an author or argument
- **Logos**, which means demonstrating specific pieces of evidence that support the text's purpose
- **Pathos**, which relates to engaging the emotions

Practice rhetorical listening:

- What is not here? Are there any notable absences? Things/people/ideas the author does not mention?
- Are there ideas or appeals that potentially challenge your acceptance of the author's work?

Although we have asked you to identify individual appeals, such rhetorical tools usually work together, and it can be hard to pull them apart. In identifying the various rhetorical components of a text, consider how they collaborate to make a text successful and persuasive . . . or not.

■ Genre Analysis

Hopefully in trying out these methods you're beginning to notice that there are lots of overlaps. Although we've offered distinctions, at their core, all of these methods are rhetorical, and they're all discursive. They all value words and suggest that they are meaningful, particularly when you consider them within context. Further, you can mix and match methods to best meet your research project. One method is termed "rhetorical analysis," because it places the rhetorical moves that an author makes in the foreground. "Content analysis" is also rhetorical, but it places a numerical accounting of certain words, phrases, or rhetorical moves in the foreground. A final method (which is also grounded in a rhetorical framing of language) to consider is **genre analysis.*** Genre is often used as a synonym for type or kind, and most of us are used to thinking about genre in terms of movies, music, and literature. For genre analysis, we'll ask you to turn your attention to the homely genres we find all around us, genres in the wild, genres that develop because of a clear rhetorical need, or **exigency**. Exigency and **genre** have a sort of problem and solution relationship. For example, consider the relationships of these exigencies and genres:

Exigency	Genre
You're hungry and want to know what you can order and how much it will cost at a restaurant	Menu
It's the beginning of the semester and you want to know what to expect in class	Syllabus
You might want to return the thing that you bought from the store, and you need proof of purchase	Receipt
You have been caught speeding, and you need to know how to pay for the penalty	Speeding Ticket

Most of us practice genre analysis every time we compose something new. For instance, the first time that you write a resume, you probably look at some examples, consider what seem to be the norms and expectations—or **conventions**—and then you choose how you might personalize or **deviate** from those in a way that is consistent with success in the genre. There are a

In using genre analysis mindfully and consistently, you work towards making your writing and research performances more consistently successful.

number of things to consider when you examine a genre. First, you might pay attention to the conventions and deviations. Then, you might consider the particular **affordances**, or what the genre allows, and **constraints**, the things the genre doesn't allow. For instance, if you're excited to go to a new restaurant, but it doesn't have an online menu, you will have to go to the restaurant to find out what your options are. A restaurant that changes their menu on a daily basis might purposefully choose not to put their menu online because the affordances and constraints of an online menu are such that you'll need to constantly change what's there to make sure that you aren't misleading potential customers. A menu on a blackboard has the affordance of being easy to change for immediate customers who are in the restaurant, but it's constrained too in that it doesn't share menu items with potential customers outside of the restaurant as a digital menu might.

Genre analysis can be powerful in helping us understand the work words do in our communities. For instance, together with a student we studied the crime notices distributed through email at our university. By looking at seven years of these warnings, we were able to see the way that the genre changed over time; it transformed from a simple notice to a specific warning

---

Try This Together: Genre Analysis (45 minutes)

With a partner, select a genre that interests you. We've named a number of them throughout this chapter, but you might also consider online reviews, tweets, recipes, game manuals, instructions, emails, or memos. Find three to five examples of artifacts within the genre. Now try identifying some of the components of the genre:

- What is the genre's exigency?
- What is the social action of the genre? What does it do?
- What are the conventions of the genre? What are features it has evolved to include? What are perhaps other features this genre has shed or left behind for good reason?
- What are the deviations in the various examples you have collected? Which are most effective and why?

Taking these findings together, what can you learn about the genre? What is the impact of the genre? How might you use this information in the future?

that encouraged members of the community to be vigilant about their safety and active in reporting suspicions. Unfortunately, given the vague information about suspects provided in the crime notices, the change in the genre had the impact of making members of the campus community feel unsafe and encouraging people to act on racial biases rather than evidence. Our analysis helped us understand this campus problem and offer strategies for confronting it.

Focus on Delivery: Developing a Coding Scheme

Now we turn to making sense of methods for examining discursive patterns by developing a **coding scheme**. There are a few ways to develop codes and to identify the emergent patterns in the corpus:

- **Deductive coding/tagging:** With this approach, you use a theoretical frame, research instrument, or established set of codes and look through your data to tag places where you see the pattern operating.

- **Inductive coding/tagging:** With this approach you develop codes based on interpretation. Instead of bringing a prescriptive set of patterns to a text and then looking for those patterns, you approach your data with openness. Then, you read, rhetorically listen to, and annotate your text. Next, as you notice connections between ideas and words in the text, you develop codes that describe those patterns. Finally, you apply these codes throughout the corpus by systematically noting each time you see the code applied.

Whichever approach you use, make sure to be consistent with your codes. To be systematic with your coding, develop a plan for identifying your codes within the corpus. There are numerous digital platforms that can help you, or you can create a coding notebook, and you might consider color-coding to make your coded data discernible. You might **triangulate** your findings by working with a partner or research team to see if they code the data in the same way that you do.

Florian Schneider suggests that you might pay attention to the following kinds of linguistic and rhetorical patterns in a text, and they may become your codes:

- **Word groups:** Be attentive to the vocabulary and syntax. Certain groups of words may demonstrate connection to a particular community, interest, or event.

- **Grammar features:** Consider pronoun usage, demonstrations of colloquial or vernacular language, and level of formality.

- **Rhetorical and literary figures:** Look for specific uses of language such as allegories, metaphors, similes, idioms, and proverbs. If you're unfamiliar with these terms, take time to look them up and find some examples.

- **Direct and indirect speech:** Identify the speaker(s) in the text. Do some of the ideas or words come from someone other than the author? If so, when? What is the effect?

- **Once you've coded your data, carefully write up your findings.** Then, it is time to make sense of what you have learned! Consider the significance of the words you have examined, their rhetorical impact, and the contextual meaning you have identified. Chapter 8 offers some different recommendations for how you might write up your findings.

■ Works Cited

Antaki, Charles, et al. "Discourse Analysis Means Doing Analysis: A Critique of Six Analytic Shortcomings." *Discourse Analysis Online*, vol. 1, no. 1, 2003. *Sheffield Hallam University*, extra.shu.ac.uk/daol/articles/v1/n1/a1/antaki2002002.html.

Aristotle. *Rhetoric*, translated by W. Rhys Roberts. *Internet Classics Archive*, classics.mit.edu/Aristotle/rhetoric.1.i.html.

Bazerman, Charles. *Shaping Written Knowledge: The Genre and Activity of the Experimental Article in Science*. 1988. The WAC Clearinghouse, 2000. wac.colostate.edu/books/landmarks/bazerman-shaping/.

Elbow, Peter. *Writing Without Teachers*. Oxford UP, 1998.

Foss, Sonja K., and Cindy L. Griffin. "Beyond Persuasion: A Proposal for an Invitational Rhetoric." *Communication Monographs*, vol. 62, no. 1, March 1995, pp. 2–18. doi.org/10.1080/03637759509376345.

Gonzalez, Jennifer. *Cult of Pedagogy*, www.cultofpedagogy.com/.

Lenssen, Paige. "The Ethics and Legality of Financial Regulation: What Enron Revealed." *Xchanges*, vol. 10, no. 2, xchanges.org/the-ethics-and-legality-of-financial-regulation-10-2-11-1.

Mckoy, Temptaous. "#IssaTrapDissertation," Socratemp.com. 2021.

Miller, Carolyn R. "Genre as Social Action." *Quarterly Journal of Speech*, vol. 70, no. 2, May 1984, pp. 151–67. *Taylor & Francis Online*, doi.org/10.1080/00335638409383686.

Ratcliffe, Krista. *Rhetorical Listening: Identification, Gender, Whiteness*. Southern Illinois UP, 2006.

Richards, I. A. *The Philosophy of Rhetoric*, Oxford UP, 1965.

Royster, Jacqueline Jones. *Traces of a Stream: Literacy and Social Change among African American Women*, U Pittsburgh P, 2000.

Schneider, Florian. "How to Do a Discourse Analysis." *Politics East Asia*, 13 May 2013, www.politicseastasia.com/studying/how-to-do-a-discourse-analysis/.

Smith, Dorothy E. "'K is Mentally Ill:' The Anatomy of a Factual Account." *Sociology*, vol. 12, no. 1, 1 January 1978, pp. 23–53. Sage Journals, doi.org/10.1177/003803857801200103.

Wardle, Elizabeth, and Doug Downs. *Writing About Writing. Bedford/St. Martins*, fourth edition, 2020.

Chapter 5. Working with People

New to town, you notice a lot of activity at a skate park near where you live. You walk nearby a time or two, noticing the activities, which involve small groups of teenagers, some of whom talk with one another and others of whom appear far more interested in attempting skateboarding feats while friends and accomplices video record.

At a local coffee shop where you frequently go to study, you begin to notice a pattern in the ways twenty-somethings sit at tables by themselves and divide their time between paying attention to their phones and paying attention to their computer screens.

You've started a new job at a local restaurant where the managers, kitchen team, and front of the house staff gather for weekly meetings. By the fourth meeting, you notice the same people talk, some of them saying the same things almost verbatim each week.

In each of these scenarios, you begin to wonder why and how people do what they do in these contexts. Questions begin to form. In this chapter, you will learn more about how researchers work with people and how they might approach such contexts.

Just as working with archives requires that we build careful stories of those who lived in the past, choosing to do research by working with people in the present requires a great degree of care. In Chapter 2, we suggested that ethical research with people begins with following your university's practices for working with human subjects. In this chapter, we discuss different research methods that can be helpful once you've determined that your research question is best answered through writing with, talking to, or observing people. As we discussed in Chapter 3, there's a lot of information already out there in secondary forms of research—literature that has already been read and reviewed, surveys that have already been conducted, sources that have already included ethnographic research in their design so that you don't have to. **Ethnography** (from the Greek *ethno-*, meaning "people" and *-grapho,* meaning "to write") is a common research methodology, a way of thinking and doing that includes many kinds of methods put together as data in the humanities and social sciences. It uses a variety of research practices that work with people in order to come to some kind of conclusion about a societal or cultural phenomenon. In order to study societies, of course, you have to work with people, which is why ethnographers use a variety of methods in their research that we cover here, like **interviews** and **surveys**, as well as some of the methods that we've talked about in earlier chapters, like coding schemes.

While you may or may not be ready to become an ethnographer, it helps to think about your research question a bit in order to determine if it might be best answered by working with people rather than in some other way.* When we conduct research about writing in particular, our first impulse may be to talk to those who are already engaged in the practice we are interested in: those who write! However, it's important to remember before we decide to work with people that many researchers who study writing have already produced a lot of knowledge on that subject by working with human subjects, whether by using focus groups to figure out if what students learn in university writing classes transfers to other classes (Bergman and Zepernick), interviewing students to see if there is a link between reading and identity (Glenn and Ginsberg), or surveying students to see how they really feel about buying a plagiarized essay online (Ritter). Lots of excellent people-based research has already been done about a variety of research topics. It's important to do some preliminary reading (this is where your worknets come in!) to figure out if you should go through the careful process of working with people or if your research question can be answered by another means. It's also important to know when the benefits of working with people outweigh any potential drawbacks. Some questions you can ask yourself as you decide if you want to work with people in research that might span a semester are:

> Because working with people also frequently takes into account their positions and situations, there may be connections worth exploring between people and places or people and things (see Chapter 6).

Try This Together: People-Focused Research (20 minutes)

Working with a partner, generate a list of three to five research focuses where people seem important to some activity, but you aren't aware of any studies related to this group, or you think the people may be difficult to gain access to. Why do you think this group hasn't been studied before? What are some of the reasons access may be challenging? What ideas do you have for ways to gain access to this person or group?

Should I work with people?* Likely YES if	Should I work with people? Likely NO if
• I want to replicate a prior study with people on a smaller scale to see if it is still true; • I want to build on prior studies by working with people; • I have insider insight into a particular group; • I want to help preserve someone's story or memory; • there is information about people's behaviors, feelings, sensations, knowledge, background, or values about my topic that I don't know and cannot find out any other way; • my ethics review and research can be completed in the time I have allotted for this work; • I want to gather pilot information on a topic rather than generate definite conclusions; or • working with people might help prove or disprove a theory.	• the research question has already been answered by many other studies and does not need replication; • I already know what I think people will answer; • I don't know anyone from the population of people who would be knowledgeable about my research question; • I won't have the time to transcribe or code a lot of data; • I have definite opinions about how people should behave or respond while I work with them; • my work will be with vulnerable people—for example, under the age of 18—or about sensitive content; • my work will put people in physical or emotional discomfort; or • I have some kind of power over the people I might work with.

The decision about whether or not to work with people should be made with care. If possible, ask other researching writers why they decided to work with people (or not).

Once you've decided that you want to work with people in order to gather data to try to answer your research question, it's important to think about the kind of method you want to use. We'll be talking about **surveys, interviews**, and **case-study** approaches to research design in this chapter, and each method has its own distinct advantages and disadvantages (often related to how much time a researcher has to work with large amounts of data). We like to think of these as differences in the **proximity**—closeness—of a researcher to her research question and how it might be best answered. A **survey** is an eagle-eye, overhead view of a group of people that gathers big-picture and multilayered information, often about a breadth of knowledge, behaviors, and opinions. **Interviews** allow for a much closer, intimate, in-depth view of one or more of those same things. A **case-study** approach might balance between near and far, using some up-close interview data or site-based observations to support parts of an argument, and using the benefit of the breadth of survey data to support other parts. As you begin to think about which method is right for you, start thinking about whether your question implies a research strategy that would be better as a snapshot from above (How stressed out does writing a paper make university students?) or as an in-depth look into particular processes (How stressed out did writing a paper make a particular student over a particular period time?).

■ Surveys

One of the ways we collect data about numbers of people that are too large to interview—depending on your time frame for data collection, this might be 20 people or it might be in the thousands—is a survey. A survey is a series of carefully-designed questions, sometimes called a **questionnaire**. In the context of a research project, surveys are put together with the intention of gathering information that will answer a bigger research question. Whether working with smaller or larger populations of people, surveys can help you determine both countable, or quantitative, information about your respondents (how many people answered yes or no on a question, for example) and descriptive information, or qualitative data, about their opinions, habits, and beliefs—what we might call **variables**.* In the following examples, we discuss how a researcher might go about research design and considerations when working with small and large groups as well as with one or more variables. However, when it comes to survey question design and survey implementation (getting your surveys out to intended respondents), there are resources that you can access that will help no matter how large or small a population you study.

Example 1: You get your most recent paper back from your instructor, and on it you've received a B+. All in all, you're pretty happy, since you've always gotten Bs on high school writing assignments. You get into a conversation after class with someone next to you who is very upset that he got a B+ on

The word "variables" is also used to describe quantitative data. Much like qualitative variables, variables in those cases are items that you can measure, such as time, height, density, distance, strength, and weight. Such variables are usually those that come with measurement markers—pounds, inches, centimeters, microns, moles.

his paper. "I've only ever gotten As on high school English papers," he says. Because of this conversation, you've become curious about how being graded on writing in high school affects people's perception of themselves as "good" writers by the time they are in college or university. A well-designed survey might look at a small relevant population of people (say, a classroom's worth. Your classroom's worth!) that would help determine both the answer to that research question and even the future pathway of a research project—perhaps after surveying 25 students, you are so interested in some answers that you'd like to follow up more closely by interviewing four or five of them. A research project of this size benefits from **convenience sampling***—finding survey participants by who you know.

What are some ethical implications of convenience sampling?

Once you know who you are going to survey, you might think about the kinds of information that would be helpful to know about the two variables you're interested in: people's feelings about themselves as writers and their feelings about grades. You might survey respondents with **open-ended questions**, which allow students to write (or say) their responses in short statements or sentences, or with **closed-ended questions**, in which students would choose among a finite set of answer choices (like "yes" or "no"). Open-ended questions better allow you to report descriptive data, while closed-ended questions allow you to get a quick snapshot of a large number of responses. Question design depends on the kind of information you need: if you need to determine what you mean by a "good" writer, you'll need to be able to define it—or determine if that's something you'll want your survey respondents to define for you. You may want to know about what kinds of grades or comments students received on high school papers and what kinds of grades or comments they've received on college or university papers. These kinds of information are well-suited to open-ended questions. However, you might also want to know how happy students are with particular grades. In order to get that information, it might be best to ask students closed-ended questions, assessing people's feelings about writing on an **ordinal scale**—an ordered set of numbers that correspond to a variable, like how happy or unhappy a student is with a particular grade on a paper. The people you're surveying should be able to distinguish between the kinds of modifiers you use to describe that variable.

For example:

I just got a B back on my last paper. On a scale of 1–5, I am
1. Extremely happy
2. Very happy
3. Somewhat happy
4. Not so happy
5. Not at all happy

Most people can figure out that in the order of things, "extremely" is higher than "very," and "not at all" is lower than "not so." The easy part about this kind of survey is that you can distribute and collect the survey in class. After you collect your survey data, you can begin to put together a picture of how the small sample group you're working with feels about the relationship between high school and college or university paper grades and how the group members feel about their writing performance. However, it would be important to compare what you find out with other studies that have been done about your topic in order to synthesize as much available data as you can in order to draw conclusions from it.

Example 2: Let's say you've been thinking a lot about a conversation you've had with your father recently. In it, he talked a lot about unpredictable weather and how it's been affecting his gardens. When you brought up the idea of global warming, he got a bit flustered and insisted that it was just a matter of weather variability. Since then, you've been thinking a lot about whether the kind of words people use to discuss climate change impacts whether or not they believe in it as a proven scientific phenomenon. After doing a bit of reading, you come across an article that talks about the kinds of questions climate-change surveys ask their respondents—Tariq Abdel-Monem and colleagues' "Climate Change Survey Measures: Exploring Perceived Bias and Question Interpretation." At the end of that article, you notice the authors mentioned that often survey respondents did not have a clear consensus about the definitions of the terms used to describe climate change. The authors call for more research on that issue in particular, which fits well with the thoughts you'd been having about the conversation with your father.

You decide to design a survey to help clarify how people interpret climate-related terms, like "weather variability," "climate change," "global warming," "greenhouse effect," and "arctic shrinkage." Because you're interested in how lots of people define these terms, you're not limiting your sample only by the convenience of who you are immediately near but on a more random sample of groups of people that begin with who you know but snowball, or grow bigger, from there: you might make a list of all possible people you could send a survey to, such as people in all of your classes, your instructors, your friends, your parents and grandparents and their friends, clubs you and your family belong to, members of a church, organization, or extracurricular activity. This list might make you decide that you are only interested in a certain **demographic** (or particular slice of the population, such as those between the ages of eighteen and twenty-five), in which case you might narrow your list to one or two groups and make sure that you have the people you survey identify their age groups in a survey question. If you just want large numbers of responses and are only mildly interested in demographic data, you might design a survey that can be distributed online and circulated widely—posted on social media, for example, or to online classroom message boards. Perhaps you would aim, in this case, to survey 100 people about their interpretation of climate-related terms.

In this example, you'll want to think about the best way to answer a specific research question about how people interpret climate-related terminology. Because there has been a lot of survey research already done in this area, your best place to start designing your survey is to look at surveys that have been conducted before—which brings us to some good advice about survey design, no matter the research question!

Try This: Writing Survey Questions (30 minutes)

Write two survey questions each for Examples 1 and 2. What underlying concept or variable are your survey questions trying to explore? How do those variables relate to the research question in each example? How do your survey questions for Example 1 (writing and grades) and Example 2 (climate change) differ according to what you're trying to find out?

■ Designing Good Questionnaires

Unlike interviews, which are often intimately tied to a research design that is so specific they usually have to be uniquely crafted, surveys are often more general. Yet, like interview questions, survey questions should be tested before they are launched in a questionnaire and you accidentally receive information you don't want! The good news is that you have access to a range of national and international surveys (and their questions) that have already been pre-tested for you: Roper iPoll through the Roper Center for Public Opinion Research (ropercenter.cornell.edu/ipoll/), the Pew Research Center (www.pewresearch.org/), Gallup (www.gallup.com/home.aspx), the Inter-University Consortium for Political and Social Research (ICPSR) (www.icpsr.umich.edu/web/pages/ICPSR/index.html), and Ipsos (www.ipsos.com/en) all store large repositories of surveys—both their analyses and the questions themselves. You can search them by keyword and find surveys on topics done that are similar to the one you're planning.

Once you have a few models of survey questions, you can change them to suit your needs. There are a few best practices to keep in mind when designing your own questionnaire:

- Don't forget instructions! Be sure to tell people briefly what they can expect (how many questions, how to fill out the survey, and how long it will take to complete).

- Questions should be clear and free of jargon: don't put in any specialized vocabulary that would be difficult for a respondent to understand.

- If you have to use technical terms, define them for your respondents.

- Each question should measure only one thing at a time—avoid questions that ask people to respond to multiple items in one question.

- If you are putting answers on a scale, respondents should have between five and seven points from which to choose.

- Be as specific as you can with your questions, whether they are open- or closed-ended.

- Questions should be short. In fact, your questionnaire should be short! When questions and surveys are too long, people lose interest and do not complete them.

- With closed-ended questions, people often choose the first option they read (if reading a survey) and the last option they hear (if a survey is read aloud). Vary the order of your answers to avoid this, if you can.

- Try to avoid loaded (or unloaded!) language that might persuade your respondents to answer a certain way: there is a perceived difference between, for example, the words "climate change" and "global warming." Be sure you use the terminology you mean, and be ready to explain your choices in your analysis.

■ Designing and Distributing Surveys

Surveys can be physically designed and distributed in a number of ways: on paper through the mail, in person, on the phone, or online through email or a distributed link. It's important to note that if you deliver a survey in person (on the phone or distributing a paper survey), you should have an introductory script that gives a framework and instructions for your research.

If you are designing and/or distributing a survey online, you can use websites that offer free survey software with some basic functionality—surveys of ten questions or less, say, or surveys that max out at a total number of respondents.* These are excellent and professional sites to use to begin your survey research, and the surveys you produce with them can be circulated and embedded into emails to specific people or circulated as a link that can be forwarded on to other people than its first recipients. If you require more functionality, you might check with your college or university's research office, some of which give access to institutional survey software to students upon request. This will enable you to design farther-reaching surveys that often have extra bells and whistles to their design and functionality, like graphic sliding scales, heat maps, and the ability to drag-and-drop text into categories.

Test your survey by sharing a draft with a friend, roommate, or classmate and listening to their feedback. Sometimes called usability testing, or user-testing, this, too, is an approach to research commonly practiced by professional and technical writers.

Try This: Revising Survey Questions (15 minutes)

Working with the questions for Examples 1 and 2 that you generated in the previous "Try This," revise your questions by following the suggestions in at least one of the best practices for writing questionnaires.

Once your survey is ready for distribution, it's important to know that a good research process should result in a high survey response rate. The larger your sample size or the less you know your targeted audience (such as in the climate change example), the lower your response rate is likely to be. In a large survey, a good response rate is about 30 percent. So, if you really wanted to survey 100 people, you would want to send your survey out to at least 300 people to try to reach that number. However, a high response rate for a small survey, such as our first example of a 25-student classroom, is about 80 per-cent—the smaller, more personal, and more targeted an audience, the higher the response rate.

Now, let's say you successfully surveyed 25 people in your classroom, but after looking at your survey results, you decide you want more information from just a few of those people. An interview might be an excellent method to achieve that purpose.

■ Interviews

Interviews allow a researcher a real-time environment that allows for things that surveys don't, like being able to ask follow-up questions or asking some-one to clarify an answer. Yet interviews also generate a lot of data because conversations need to be recorded and usually transcribed or written down (and it takes about three hours to transcribe every one hour of talk). A bene-fit to interviews is that there are different types, depending on your research question. You might sit down with a small group of people, called a **focus group**, and ask one question to see how people respond and negotiate their answers in groups, since usually one person's response provokes agreement, disagreement, or room for follow-up. A focus group might enable you to get a general sense of consensus or understand divergent attitudes about a particular variable. You might develop questions for **1-on-1 research interviews**, in which you sit down with one person at a time and ask them a series of carefully-designed questions that help you answer your research question (you might repeat the same set of questions with each interview for consistency, in this case). If your purposes extend beyond only answering a research question and you are trying to preserve a sound recording of stories or memories for future generations to listen to, then you would conduct an **oral history interview** with either one person or a group of people, in which you would design an interview script with topics about a particular area of interest and a long list of questions that you may or may not ask, depending on your participant's memory and willingness to talk. Unlike a research interview, an oral history interview does not seek to replicate the same questions for each interviewee but instead trusts the process of proceeding through topics and questions that result in the best outcome: an oral history of a person, place, or group.

■ Asking Questions "From the Side"

Some of the same advice about survey questions applies to interview questions: They should be clear, specific, short, and free of specialized vocabulary your interviewees might not know. They shouldn't try to double up a few questions in just one breath or be written in a way that offends a listener or presumes something about them. However, unlike survey questions, interviews don't really benefit from closed-ended (yes or no) questions; usually you are more interested in *why* a participant answered yes or no.

Good interviews come from really good questions that are related to your research question, but research questions often are not what you would actually ask someone in an interview. In other words, there is a difference between your research question and an interview question. The best way to ask about your research question is actually by asking an interview question from the side rather than head on. For example, a research question about a topic you want to learn about—let's say, plagiarism—is not best answered by the most direct question. Asking, "Have you ever copied a paper from someone?" likely would result in some discomfort on both sides of the interviewing table. Instead, designing questions from the side might be a better way to get at what you're hoping to find out. In the case of curiosity about plagiarism, you might ask about someone's knowledge of online paper mills, ask about whether or not they have ever had trouble with their works cited page, ask about their opinion of plagiarism detection software, or ask if they know about campus resources that help students revise their work. All of these topics are about plagiarism without developing an accusatory tone about serious academic misconduct, and they would probably help you establish a more interesting angle for your own research question once you've spoken to a few people.

Try This: Designing Interview Questions from the Side (30 minutes)

In order to design an interview question from the side, you'll need to know your research question. (Note that Chapter 1 introduces research questions and the ways they expand and shift throughout a research process.) Once you have that, you'll need to figure out what exactly it is you're hoping to learn to be able to answer that research question. Then, you'll need to determine who you might ask to get at what you want to learn. Finally, you'll generate a list of interview questions that would help you get at what you're trying to learn—from the side! Here's an example of how this process works:

- **Research Question:** What matters more in the workplace: "hard skills" (technical skills) or "soft skills" (communication skills)?

- **What I'm hoping to learn:** Do employers value technical skills more than communication skills or vice-versa? Are college or university graduates being given the tools they need in technical and communication skills to get a job when they graduate? Which kind of skill is the more difficult to learn?

- **Who might have this information:** Employers/employees at any company, recently employed college or university graduates, instructors in both technical and communication-based fields are all likely to have insights.

- **Interview questions from the side that will help me learn what I want to know:**
    - For an employer: What is the most important skill an employee can have?
    - For a student: What is the hardest assignment you ever had to complete? What made it so hard?
    - For anyone: Think about a recent problem that came up in your workplace. What do you think caused it?

Based on this example, come up with some interview questions from the side for your own research question.

■ Interviewing Equipment and Best Practices

Unlike surveys, to really be useful, interviews need to be audio- or video-recorded and then transcribed so you can understand what was said in order to interpret your data. This means that interviews require putting in some effort to be successful: finding a comfortable and quiet place to meet (so that voices are easily heard over any ambient noise), using a good quality audio and/or video recorder, and finding the time it takes to listen and transcribe the voices you hear (including your own). As you decide which kind of interview to conduct, you'll want to consider that transcribing a 1-on-1 research or oral history interview is much easier than transcribing a group interview, where people talk over and interrupt one another. Similarly, in a video recording, it is easier to set up a camera that captures two people in a frame than a whole group, which may require another person to operate a camera. While we don't expect you to bring a camera crew to a group interview, it's important to know the benefits and constraints of working with certain kinds of equipment.

When it comes time to conduct the actual interview, you'll want to talk to your interviewees before you begin recording. About a week or so before, it

---

Try This Together: Interview Question Sketch (30 minutes)

In a small group, choose one of the following topics:

- Fake news
- Seasonal affective disorder
- Photo retouching
- Learning a second language
- Genetically modified foods

Next, complete the following steps:

1. Develop a research question about your chosen topic.
2. Decide what you would hope to learn from interviews.
3. Consider who might have the information you need.
4. Write three interview questions you might ask.

A Deed of Gift is a separate and special document from other consent forms. In a Deed of Gift, the oral history participant "gifts" the interviewer (or institution, or library, or archive) their story so that other people may listen to it or use it for research purposes.

is often good practice to share the interview questions or interview script (in the case of an oral history, which might be more loosely configured) with your participant(s) so they know what you plan on asking and thus can be prepared with thoughtful answers. This isn't always possible, especially if you don't have a way of contacting your interviewees beforehand. The day of your interview, you should make sure that your participants know the details of where you'll be meeting and at what time. Right before your interview, you should discuss with your interviewee the **ethics protocol** of the interview in order to get their **informed consent**, as we discussed in Chapter 2. If you're undertaking an oral history interview, you will also want to discuss a **deed of gift*** with your interviewee, in which they agree to release their story both to you and to a larger public repository of other stories like theirs. This is unlike a research interview, in which it is likely that only you will ever listen to the recording

---

Try This Together: Research Interview vs. Oral History Interview (45 minutes)

Because a research interview is very different in its purpose (to help answer a research question) than an oral history interview (which records and preserves stories and memories and sometimes helps to answer a research question), it's important that interview questions are designed with the appropriate purpose in mind depending on the type of interview you're conducting. Because they emphasize storytelling, ways of seeing the self or the community, and memories of historical events, oral history interviews often need fewer specific questions and more prompts than research interviews.

First, choose one of the following topics:

- Changes in telephone technology since its patent in 1876
- The best cake you've ever eaten
- The "millenium" or "Y2K" bug
- The development of a local community center in your region
- The increase in diabetes since 1980
- The price of gasoline over the last 100 years

Then, generate with a partner four different interview questions (one of which needs to be a follow-up question) for both a research interview and an oral history interview. When you're finished, discuss the differences between the two sets of questions and what accounts for these differences.

or read a transcript. After any kind of interview, you'll want to follow up with your interviewees with a brief note of thanks that reminds them of what will happen with their data as well as how they might reach you if they have questions about the interview process.

When you're interviewing, it's important to keep track of your main research question, as responses may stray from what you expect and you might get caught up in what your interviewee is saying. It's important to be prepared with **follow-up interview questions** that might piggy-back off of a prior question. Similarly, you might also want to be prepared to ask "Why?" or "Tell me more about that," after an answer you receive (especially if you get an answer that is shorter than you expect). Sometimes the best questions simply ask for clarification ("Could you tell me what you mean by that?" or "Could you give me an example of what you mean?") or are constructed on the fly ("Can we go back to that example you talked about earlier?" or "How did you feel about that?"). Oral history interviews benefit from mocking up an outline of topics and then generating a list of many possible questions in each section of your outline and letting the interview organically emerge from whatever series of questions are appropriate.

Finally, it is important to take into account that, as the interviewer, you develop and ask the questions. This places you in a position of power (even if you don't feel particularly powerful, such as if you are a student interviewing an instructor). When you interview someone, you enter into a relationship with them for a brief time, and it is important that everyone feels as comfortable as possible.

■ Putting It All Together: Case Studies

A **case study** is a kind of qualitative research method that combines data collected from a variety of other methods that we have already talked about—like surveys, interviews, and different kinds of documents and artifacts. A case-study approach to answering a research question is best suited when the phenomenon you're studying is particular, or distinct, in relation to a larger society, culture, or environment. You might want to look at a case to understand broader details than any one method, like an interview with one person, might tell you. Looking at cases is particularly helpful when researchers are trying to gain some insight about the nature of a particular environment in more detail; however, it's important to note that the limitation of a case study is that one single, detailed instance of a phenomenon cannot be used to generalize to all instances of that kind of activity everywhere. Case studies offer us a snapshot of an individual unit, a glimpse as comprehensive as we can get, that helps us understand or know systems of the world—and its people—a bit better.

To undertake a case study, you will need to gather one or more kinds of data that we have already discussed and then analyze or code it to find categories or patterns. Once you have those preliminary analyses or codes, you might compare what you've found with other, similar cases. Finally, you'll work to interpret your research notes to come to some conclusions about how the case you've chosen offers up an understanding of your research question.

For example, let's say commencement is right around the corner and you are interested in the rules and regulations that govern graduation—what people can (and cannot) wear, what freedom they have to decorate their mortarboard hats or wear culturally significant accessories, how honorary degrees get conferred and taken away—and what graduation signifies in terms of a major life event for college or university students. In other words, you are seeking an answer to a broad research question, "What does commencement *mean* to a college or university community?" Because most colleges and universities engage in this activity, choosing to look at one—at the college or university

---

Try This: Case Study Planning (30 minutes)

Using the commencement example above, develop design considerations for a case study by answering the following questions:

- What kinds of data will you collect?
- What are the best methods to use to collect your data?
- Who should you talk to?
- What other cases can you compare this case to?
- What are you going to look for in your data? What are your variables?

you attend—would offer a case-study glimpse at the nature of commencement. Your examination of commencement at your institution would give an audience some ways to understand how graduation is significant to college and university communities.

You might begin this case study with a worknet, reviewing the literature about the history of commencements, recent newsworthy pieces about dress codes or cultural items that have made it into the popular press, and local updates from your college or university about the who, what, where, and how of commencement planning. Once you've done some reading, it's time to plan your case study: just what kind of data should you collect, from who, and why?

We realize that even planning out a case study as a brief exercise might seem overwhelming, especially if you have to use one or more research methods to get there. That's why it's important at every step in your research process—whether gathering a preliminary round of survey results, reflecting after an interview or site-based observation, or handling a new artifact—to document what you notice, document what sticks out during the experience you've just had, document how it connects to other data-collection or data-handling experiences, and document what significant patterns emerge as your research experiences add up. Researchers call this documentation a **research memo,**[*] and it will help you move from data collection to data interpretation—in other words, a research memo will help you begin to make sense of all the information you are gathering in a way that is not as overwhelming as looking at data from 50 surveys, 5 interviews, and 3 site visits all at once.

> Research memos are also remarkably important for showing the work and communicating in-progress analysis when multiple researchers collaborate.

Focus on Delivery: Writing a Research Memo

A research memo is an in-between phase of writing: it's not the same as the data you collect or code, but it also isn't a final research paper. Instead, it's an analytic memo that a researcher writes after each of their major data-collection episodes to help them make sense of what they just experienced. It helps a researcher look back on the small pieces of what they've done to understand emergent patterns for analysis of their research question. Because all of the small parts of a case-study—field notes, transcriptions, documents, coding sheets—can add up, taking time out to review and reflect is necessary.

Unlike the observant, real-time detail that is required of field notes, research memos are instead a place for analysis, which means they are a place for freewriting, thinking on paper, noting patterns and anomalies by comparing one kind of data with another, assessing your progress or noting problems with your research, planning for a future stage, and noting your feelings about your research. You might think of a research memo as a working paper about the major data points of your case study—this may mean one interview or a series of interviews, one site visit or multiple visits, one coding sheet or ten coding sheets. Regardless, it's important to keep up with your research memos, as they will simplify the process of interpreting multiple kinds of data.

As you write your research memo, it is best if you have with you the data you've already collected (the interview transcript, field notes, coding sheet, document, or artifact).

In your research memo, you should

- include relevant dates and data types (e.g., "June 14 research memo on interview with Sonja Notte, May 31") and bibliographic information if a textual source;

- include relevant quotations (for interviews or surveys), quantities (for surveys), observations (for fieldwork), words and phrases (for coded documents), or descriptions (for material artifacts) that stick out to you from your data collection;

- record why you think these chosen details are important, relevant, or stick out;

- reflect on how the data contributes to clarifying your research question or helps to define or refine the scope of your research question (this can help you revise your **research proposal**); and

- comment on what you think of the data: What questions do you have? What patterns or trends are emerging when you consider this data in light of others you've collected? What connections can you make across data sets? What confuses you?

■ Works Cited

Abdel-Monem, Tariq, et al. "Climate Change Survey Measures: Exploring Perceived Bias and Question Interpretation." *Great Plains Research*, vol. 24, no. 2, 2014, pp. 153–68. Project Muse, doi.org/10.1353/gpr.2014.0035.

Bergman, Linda S., and Janet S. Zepernick. "Disciplinarity and Transfer: Students' Perceptions of Learning to Write." *WPA: Writing Program Administration,* vol. 31, no. 1–2, 2007, pp. 124–49, associationdatabase.co/archives/31n1-2/31n1-2bergmann-zepernick.pdf.

Glenn, Wendy J., and Ricki Ginsberg. "Resisting Readers' Identity (Re)Construction across English and Young Adult Literature Course Contexts." *Research in the Teaching of English*, vol. 51, no. 1, 2016, pp. 84–105. National Council of Teachers of English, library.ncte.org/journals/rte/issues/v51-1/28686.

Ritter, Kelly. "The Economics of Authorship: Online Paper Mills, Student Writers, and First-Year Composition." *College Composition and Communication,* vol. 56, no. 4, 2005, pp. 601–31.

Chapter 6. Working with Places and Things

So far in this book, we've been paying close attention to words and how to do things that are ethical, meaningful, and methodical with them. In Chapter 2, we learned about how using citation systems and institutional reviews are ways of ethically planning for and representing the people and ideas we are working with. In Chapter 3, we talked about affinity and choric worknets, how words on a page can form relationships between people over time, and how words can construct inventive worlds we hadn't thought about before. In Chapter 4, we introduced coding and analysis and worked on developing a methodical research design that helps us understand the patterns that develop in language. In Chapter 5, we considered how and when to include people in our research. In this chapter, we focus on the *where** of working with words and people: where you might find words that matter, where you might go to understand that words happen in particular places and are used by particular people with particular materials, and the wheres you can create in your own primary research that are worth exploring. This chapter will give you some options for deciding if archives, site-based observing, or mapmaking are good choices for you to use to answer the research question(s) you began working with in Chapter 1. Considering these methods might also give rise to new questions you want to work with.

You might be wondering why place matters in writing, or why we should care about things if we are primarily working with words. The short answer is because *where* people are, and the things they are surrounded by, matter to the kinds of writing they produce and the subjects they care about. Places and things help build a particular rhetorical situation, and those situations create knowledge problems that we, as researchers, might solve. The longer answer might be imagined with a few examples of interesting knowledge problems that emerge when we consider how words are complicated by places and things:

- How safe is the place you live? How does the ability to walk in your neighborhood at certain times of day reinforce or detract from feeling safe? [working with places]

Whether working in archives, observing specific sites, or mapping individual spaces, considering the places where language happens and the things we use to understand those activities is a central part of being a researcher.

- What happens when we look for a source using the library's online catalogue compared to walking around and navigating the stacks? [working with places]

- What is the experience of reading an ebook or PDF compared to a printed book? What sights, sounds, feelings, and smells do you associate with each one? [working with things]

- How does it feel to read a recipe and then join a family member or friend in making your favorite dish the way you've always eaten it? [working with things]

- What might be the experience of reading love letters between two people who lived a hundred years ago compared to reading a romantic textual exchange on someone's phone today? [working with places and things]

- What changes when you use a nature identification app to learn about local plants or animals and then try to identify the nature around you on a walk to campus or in your neighborhood? [working with places and things]

- How does reading a job preparation manual differ from being on a job site? How are experiences, equipment use, and safety changed by going to a job versus reading about work? [working with places and things]

Each of these situations ask us to consider words in conjunction with places and things—how words are shaped by our experiences with places; how our bodies feel at a desk or perusing shelves; or how a walk in the woods, a meal in a kitchen, or a visit to a job site might impact our feelings about the words we use or the words we read.

Try This: Identifying Campus Trees (60 minutes)

Take a walk around or nearby your campus, noting how many and what kinds of trees you find. Write down important tree details: how tall they are, how their leaves are shaped (or whether they have leaves during the season you observe them), where they are planted, and what they smell like. Write down the names of the trees you know, and use a nature identification app to help you find out the names you don't.

In this chapter, we pay special attention to the way places invoke our senses—sight, sound, touch, smell, taste—and the way involvement of our senses shapes our research. We also look at the role things play in our research questions and research designs as well as the kind of **rhetorical weight*** they lend to our data as we fully examine our research question.

■ Methods Can Be Material

If we remember the definition of research methods from Chapter 1, that is, that they are the tools, instruments, practices, and processes that help us answer our research questions, it's important to recognize that some methods that help us think through and answer those questions are actual things themselves, whether we make them ourselves or use instruments to help us collect our data. Researchers from a variety of disciplinary backgrounds use the process of making using things as a vital part of their research methods. Take, for example, the way that making a textile, like a basket or a quilt, helps give our bodies a particular kind of touch knowledge. When we engage in sharing that basket or quilt with others and observe their reactions to our efforts, that gives us a certain kind of affective, embodied, or feeling-knowledge. It is possible that the only way to really answer a research question about how baskets or quilts make us feel or what significance they have for a community is by engaging in the material making. Thus, even seemingly ordinary practices like basket making or quilting can be a research method if they help provide knowledge about a research question.

Similarly, working with instruments as things helps us extend our knowledge to answer research questions in different ways. Perhaps, after trying to identify trees on your campus using all of your senses, you are interested in trees and the different ways they make us feel about the environments we live in. As a continuation of the "Try This" that invites you to explore campus grounds with particular attention to trees, you might move forward in such an investigation with a campus tree survey, even using satellite maps to locate where all of the trees are on your campus and visiting and taking pictures at each of those places to count how many trees exist where you spend so much

While we can't exactly put rhetoric on a scale to know what it weighs, we can think of rhetorical weight as a metaphor for significance, or the ways that our focus on important concepts may be changed by the way data is considered or presented.

time each day (see Chapter 7). Following your making of a campus tree survey, even if limited to a small section of campus, you might then, as part of your research design (see Chapter 5), create a questionnaire about how people feel about nature on campus. You also might look at the way researchers have used a variety of instruments and tools to measure this same phenomenon, for example through the use of small microphones and surface transducers (speakers) embedded in the bark of trees to give rise to projects like the Listen-Tree project (listentree.media.mit.edu/), in which people can listen to the sonic vibrations trees make in forests, or the Danish Living Tree project (airlab.itu .dk/the-living-tree), in which researchers placed small, hidden speakers in trees to allow people around them to listen differently to the life of trees represented sonically: the sounds of insects crawling, or the tree "breathing" as people get closer to it. In those particular cases, things—both instruments (microphones and speaker) and non-humans (trees)—help us understand different facets of the research question in ways that reading a literature review about the coniferous and deciduous trees in our area might not. It's important to recognize that research methods engage places, things, and texts in sometimes complicated ways and that sometimes texts themselves may be things: images, recordings, and **ephemera**—those things we never imagine might be collected and given meaning, like ticket stubs, receipts, flyers, buttons, and letters.

■ Archival Methods

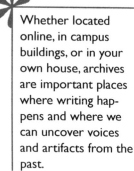

Whether located online, in campus buildings, or in your own house, archives are important places where writing happens and where we can uncover voices and artifacts from the past.

One of the ways that writers conduct primary research is by going to **original sources***—sources unlike the **secondary sources** discussed in Chapter 3, such as books and articles, that we usually find at the library or through a database search. Original sources are singular (one-of-a-kind) and provide first-hand accounts of events. They are also known as **primary sources**. One of the main places a researcher can find original sources are in archives—collections of materials such as images, texts, or audio and video recordings that are housed in one place and usually catalogued and ordered in a way that helps researchers locate the sources they want to work with. Thus, archival research methods are shaped by considering history and how it can be built out of a collection of things.

There are a few different kinds of archives, and some of them are accessed easily and from the comfort of your own home. Internet or **digital archives** are growing daily: a quick search will tell you that archival materials are available in their entirety about subjects as varied as literacy narratives (www.thedaln.org/), nature images (desertmuseum.org/center/digital_library.php), or AIDS activism (www.actuporalhistory.org/), to name a few. There are a number of websites devoted to putting many portals of digital archives in one place, notably the Digital Public Library of America (dp.la/).

What distinguishes a digital archive from a physical one is often access: some archives only digitize some content rather than all content, and some digital archives have no real physical home. Physical archives, or **traditional archives**, are usually housed in brick-and-mortar places: public libraries, universities and colleges, corporations, governments, museums, or historical societies. When they're grouped together, the sources located in archives are called **fonds** (pronounced fon), which tells you they are grouped in a specific way by the people—archivists—who put them together. Navigating the fonds is some of the most difficult (and rewarding!) work of archival research, and it often takes more time than other kinds of research. Much as working with a new computer program isn't intuitive unless you've made the program yourself, often you either have to think like someone else to navigate the fonds or let a bit of serendipity lead the way. The most important things to know about conducting archival research are the following: every archive is different and comes with different rules (which are useful to know ahead of time), most archives utilize some kind of **finding aid**—a description that places the material in context—to help researchers use them, and most archives are staffed with **archivists**—people who can help you navigate the archives so that you can find what you think you're looking for. We say "think you're looking for" because in many cases, archival work is more about what you don't find when you're expecting to, or what you do find when you aren't!

Archival research isn't an exact science: often materials are labeled differently than you would label them or filed in one of any number of ways (for example, a letter about the Old Faithful geyser between two rangers in a historic Yellowstone Park archive might be filed under the rangers' names, under

Try This: Working with a Digital Archive (45 minutes)

Locate a digital archive that originates from a place close to where you are—in the same city, state, or region. Find one artifact in the archive (image, text, audio, video) and answer the following questions about it:

- What kind of artifact is it? Who authored it and for what purpose?

- What does the kind of artifact it is tell you about what it contains? How does the artifact type (for example, interview transcript, photograph, or meeting note) give you clues as to what it can contain and what it cannot?

- Why was the artifact created and by whom was it made? What function did/does it serve?

- Who was the intended audience for the artifact? Do you think the creator ever intended you to be viewing the artifact?

- When was the artifact created? What was going on in the world then that could have affected its creation?

- Where was the artifact created? Did it have to travel to be included in the archive? What does that tell you about the artifact?

- What clues from the artifact (words, formality or informality of tone or dress, position of landmarks or commonplaces) help you understand where it comes from?

- Is the artifact unique, or is it one of a series of other artifacts like it? How do you know?

- How reliable is the artifact? How do you know? How would you cite this artifact?

- Who is missing from the artifact, and what might that tell you about the time or place it was made?

- What is your own reaction to the artifact? How does it make you feel? Which of your senses are engaged by the artifact?

- What questions do you have about the artifact?

Once you have generated the answers to these questions, do one of the following:

- Draft a research proposal (see Chapter 1) that creates a research question about this artifact and uses archival research as a method; OR

- Write a rhetorical analysis (see Chapter 4) of this artifact.

"Old Faithful," or under miscellaneous letters). The key to archival research is being patient, being flexible, and knowing that it may take one or more return trips. Some tips for visiting traditional archives are:

- **Research the archives in advance.** Sometimes you have to request materials a few days in advance of your arrival or have a special pass to visit them. You can also usually locate the particular finding aids that an archive uses to help you find or request what you're looking for ahead of time.

- **Plan what to bring.** Many archives do not allow you to bring computers or cell phones and allow a pencil and paper only for notetaking. How might this affect your research process?

- **Know the costs.** If you either cannot or are not allowed to take photos of the archival materials, many archives offer printing services, but these often come at a price.

A final type of archive is a **personal archive**—a collection of materials that might be housed with you, a friend, or a relative. Perhaps your grandmother kept a collection of quilting fabric, quilts that she made, and quilting books that is in a box or closet that you know of. Or maybe your aunt has amassed a large assortment of baseball memorabilia including newspaper clippings of her favorite teams, thousands of cards, jerseys, and signed baseballs. It is also conceivable that you have been keeping a written record of your goings-on for the last fifteen years, from report cards to journals to artwork to emails. While cataloguing these personal archives would take far more work than simply going to an archive and using a finding aid, they are rich sources of research

---

Try This: Identifying a Personal Collection (1 hour)

Bring to class a personal collection of things. You may not think of old notebooks, pictures, or digital spaces as archives, but they hold information about your past, about who you were at a different time in your life. Turn your analytical eye to the archive and use primary research methods to make sense of who you were and what artifacts you developed or collected at that time. Using labels, ordering, and framing documents, curate and order artifacts from your collection, giving each piece meaning as part of a whole archive.

that allow you to engage more deeply with the contexts and places that artifacts have emerged from in ways that reading about them in a textbook would not. To that end, what separates an archive from a pile of stuff is the meaning that we give it by **curation**—the way we select, order, and label items in a way that gives shape to the significance of the collection.

One part of working with archives is caring for the people you come in contact with, even if you have never met those people who were involved with the artifacts you've found—or even if they are long gone. How might you represent in an ethical way an image, a set of correspondence, or a relationship that appears in the archives? It's important to think of uncovering the primary research of the archives that others may or may not have looked at closely as a way of honoring stories that have been there before we get to them. Whether this means we tell partial stories (perhaps we leave the part about our aunt's baseball boyfriend out of our archival story), spend time carefully constructing the contexts for artifacts (as in the case of marginalized groups, such as prison inmate records in the New York State Archive, or those records in Ireland's National Archive of women forced to give babies up for adoption by the Catholic church in the late 1960s), or reflect on our own connection with those we learn from in the archives, it is important to remember that what we find in the archives brings a past place into a present one—and that you are the person responsible for handling those places with care.

■ Site-Based Observations

Although archival work with artifacts, materials, and things asks that we pay special attention to understanding and piecing together a historical past, **site-based observations**, often called **fieldwork** or **field methods**, emphasize how close reading of sites helps us more deeply engage with a particular present. Site-based observations are an important part of qualitative research because they depend on a researcher's experience to explain a phenomenon and result in **thick description**—detailed notes—that help emplace a reader in the research while providing evidence about a particular activity or situation that the researcher has experienced.

Central to site-based observations is selecting a site that will give you more information about your research question than only reading the literature about it will tell you. For example, if you are curious about how often texting gets in the way of a person's everyday life, you could read studies about technology and distraction to gather some preliminary ideas about it. But if you wanted to generate your own primary research that could help answer that question, you might select a busy campus spot for a certain amount of time—say, two hours—and observe how often texting impacts people's ability to walk, multitask, cross a street, or interact with others. By writing down what you see in detailed field notes, you will also have **observational data** that will help you answer your research question.

However, site-based observation isn't just sitting down and recording what you see. Selection of a site, subjects (or people), activities, and things that you record should have some definable reason behind why those and not others, and it's important to spend some time thinking about your choices of site before you begin fieldwork. From the example above, where is the best spot for learning about texting and walking? Who is most likely to be engaging in the behavior you wish to observe? Why is the activity and site you've chosen the best representative of what you're trying to explore—for example, why use site-based observation when you might instead survey people about texting and distraction? What assumptions do you already have about texting and distraction that could impact how you represent it in your field notes?

Try This Together: Classroom Site-Based Observation and Comparing Field Notes (45 minutes)

During a regularly scheduled class time, devote the first 20 minutes with your classmates to treating your classroom like a field site. While your instructor teaches class, keep a field notebook of what happens, recording both informational and personal responses to the class. At the end of the 20 minutes, compare your notes with a peer's notes. Which events, details, and sensations were similar? Which were different? How could these similarities and differences be tied to the way you chose to take field notes? What did your note taking strategies allow you to notice, and what did they force you to miss? Discuss as a class what some of the best note taking strategies were for maintaining accuracy, detailing what happened, and recording personal reactions.

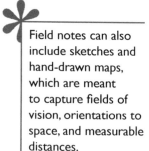

Field notes can also include sketches and hand-drawn maps, which are meant to capture fields of vision, orientations to space, and measurable distances.

Once you've generated some ideas about your chosen site and research question and gathered the permission you need (if you're working with human subjects; see Chapter 5), it's time to keep **field notes***—detailed observations about your chosen site that will help others have a rich view of a particular place. Field notes depend on your ability to be a close observer of what you see: detail people, places, and things; document sounds, smells, textures, feelings, weather conditions, tastes, colors; and define as closely as you can elements that others might not understand or share (for example, instead of "she wrote slowly" you might write "it took the writer ten minutes to compose her first sentence"). There are a few different ways to keep field notes, but we encourage you to keep a special notebook that is lightweight and portable and that you use only for site-based observations.

Many site-based observations take the form of a **double-entry journal** (see Figure 6.1) that in some way splits your notes into two columns, one side that documents an informational record of what is happening, and the other side that contains a more personal response to what is happening. These might be split and labeled "information" and "personal" or "record" and "response," and they are a good way to begin to think about the difference between what is happening and what you feel about what is happening around you.

But once you delve into a site, especially if you return to the same site more than once, you'll need to develop your own system for detailing, documenting, and defining what you see. Often there is so much happening in a place that it is difficult to know where to begin notetaking: Which conversation soundbyte is important? Does the weather or the time of day matter? What happens if you're feeling sick that day on the site? Because every site is filled with rich detail, and every researcher might take different field notes about the same moment, it's important for you to develop a system for your note taking that will help you later connect your observations to your research question. We suggest that whatever form your field notes take, you aim for the following:

- **Accuracy:** record the same kinds of information during every observational visit (date, time, location).

- **Detail:** record the who, what, where of every visit (conversation bits, room or site conditions and description, length of time it takes for something to happen).

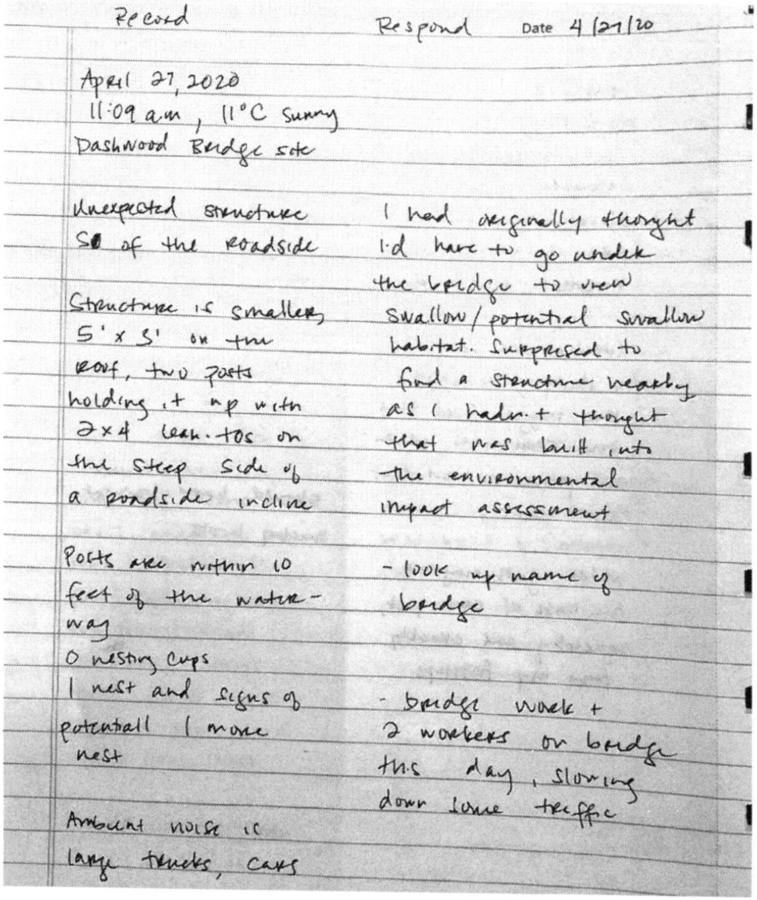

Record

April 27, 2020
11:09 a.m, 11°C Sunny
Dashwood Bridge site

Unexpected structure
S of the roadside

Structure is smaller,
5' x 3' on the
roof, two posts
holding it up with
2x4 lean-tos on
the steep side of
a roadside incline

Posts are within 10
feet of the water-
way
0 nesting cups
1 nest and signs of
potential 1 more
nest

Ambient noise is
large trucks, cars

Respond Date 4/27/20

I had originally thought
I'd have to go under
the bridge to view
swallow/potential swallow
habitat. Surprised to
find a structure nearby
as I hadn't thought
that was built into
the environmental
impact assessment

- look up name of
bridge

- bridge work +
2 workers on bridge
this day, slowing
down some traffic

Figure 6.1. Example of a double-entry journal for field notes. The left-hand column is labeled "record." The right-hand column is labeled "respond."

- **Definition:** be as specific as you can about elements around you that would help someone unfamiliar with the site understand what is happening.
- **Sensation and Response:** make note of specific ways your body feels in the space and which emotions arise.
- **Questions:** record any questions you are left with while at the site.

It's important to keep in mind that site-based observation is a source of data, and that, in order to answer your research question, your data needs to be filtered and organized in ways that account for what your question is asking.

You may well end up with more observational data than you need—but as you go back through your notes, you will begin to see patterns and trends emerging from your observations, much like when you developed your coding scheme for discourse in Chapter 4. As you compose research memos from each site visit (see Chapter 5), certain details will become important as you group similar things together, examine outliers from what you expected, or reflect on your own reactions and feelings to what you saw. All of those ways of assembling information provide evidence for answering your research question and for understanding the way that places shape what happens within them.

 # Places and Things Converge: Mapmaking as a Method

So far, we've discussed some important places where words work to make history (archives) as well as a method for recording the current impacts that places have (site-based observations). Archival research and fieldwork are privileged by researchers in both the humanities and social sciences, but they both make meaning out of observation primarily by using words. As we introduce this final method, mapmaking, we do so not because we expect you to be geographers or cartographers when you graduate, but because sometimes we see relationships and patterns more clearly when we view them spatially and visually, not only verbally or textually. Maps enable us to travel to places we've never been, and global satellite imagery allows us to

---

Try This Together: Analyzing Maps (30 minutes)

Go to *The Decolonial Atlas* (decolonialatlas.wordpress.com/) and "40 Maps that Will Help You Make Sense of the World" (twistedsifter.com/2013/08/maps-that-will-help-you-make-sense-of-the-world/) online. With a partner, choose five different maps from these sites. What are we supposed to pay attention to based on what the maps highlight? What would each map be good for? What would each map not be helpful for?

view the world from a bird's-eye view. For this reason, researchers in many disciplines rely on maps to help them understand, explore, and answer their research questions.

Making maps helps us see differently. Maps can be used to help us plan information, as in an idea map during pre-writing stages, or they can help us step back from a phenomenon so that we can see patterns and relationships at a distance, as word cloud maps do. Mapping may be part of how we compose field notes in order to orient ourselves or others to our places of research. Mapping as a method is a way of generating data visually and spatially that helps us understand focal points, themes, and hierarchies.

Mapping can also be a way of visualizing location and movement of people and things over time. For instance, let's say that you're working with the research question we raised in the beginning of the chapter about the differences and similarities between reading love letters between two people who lived a hundred years ago and reading a romantic textual exchange on someone's phone today. While you might begin your project with worknets and researching what has been written about the genres of letters and texts, mapping the location and movement of specific letters and texts might give you some different insight about the function of each that could help you answer your research question.

Try This: Map Comparison (45 minutes)

First, hand-draw a map of the trees that you found on or near your campus when you completed the "Try This: Identifying Campus Trees" exercise earlier in this chapter.

Then, consider that the process of moving back and forth between being in a the physical location and looking at a map or satellite view is called ground-truthing among geographers and cartographers. Ground-truthing cares for the ethical coordination of the direct sensory experience (finding trees on campus, as you did) and checking those impressions against the aerial imagery, satellite view, or perhaps a map you have created. Ground-truthing acknowledges that maps, too, warrant ethical consideration and that maps change because the material world changes.

Finally, compare your notes from the "Try This: Identifying Campus Trees" activity with both the map you made and a satellite view of the trees on or near your campus. What is similar? What is different?

Let's say you're working with the publicly published letters of lifelong partners Simone de Beauvoir (who lived from 1908–1986) and Jean-Paul Sartre (who lived from 1905–1980), whose correspondence spanned from 1930–1963. Let's also say you'll be working with a series of a three-month-long text exchange between you and your romantic partner. There are many ways you could begin to try to answer this research question. On the one hand, you could use some quantitative methods to help you understand these genres of exchange—you might count how many letter exchanges each participant had in each genre and compare the counts, or you might count how many letters were exchanged in three months' time and compare that number to the number of text messages exchanged in the same amount of time. Or, you might use a qualitative method by reading a sample of letters and texts and creating a coding sheet for discourse analysis (see Chapter 4) that suggests some common (or uncommon) themes that appear in both kinds of exchanges. On the other hand, you might map out these exchanges. You might place each letter in a mapped location of the place where they were at the time they were mailed, which might reveal interesting points of comparison and contrast. Based on your knowledge of where de Beauvoir and Sartre lived between 1930 and 1963, you might find that their correspondence covered the time period of the Second World War and spanned locations throughout France and Germany when Sartre was a prisoner of war. You might also chart where you and your partner lived in the three-month timespan of your exchange, accounting also for the location of text messages in space, pinging off of satellites. In this way, you are creating a location-based, or spatial, map of time travel, distance, and discourse that might help you draw some different kinds of conclusions about letters and texts in the context of a romantic relationship and in the context of the past and present.

Try This: Mapping Movement (60 minutes plus 1 day)

Try making your own map of time travel. In one 24-hour time period, document on a map of your choice where you've traveled. On either a hand-drawn or online map and using locative images (dots, lines, and arrows), reference where you were at what time of day during that 24 hours. What different information do you generate when you capture your day on a map rather than on a calendar or daily schedule of appointments?

Maps not only help us see differently—in both words and images—but they also can lead us to different kinds of realizations about our research and can exist as important research methods to help us consider elements of distance, scale, scope, and movement. To that end, they should be seen as a complementary method to site-based observations and hold much potential for being included in your field notes. Maps can also help us recognize patterns, themes, or focal points, and they can be created for audiences to help them understand, navigate, or replicate a particular research site or process.

Focus on Delivery: Curating a Collection

Whether you are working with a personal collection, a library archive, or a collection of field notes or maps, inquiry into places and things frequently requires assembling and curating a collection. Curation explores various groupings and patterns, and it often assigns numbering or naming systems so all items in the collection can be referenced. Curated collections aid in making research materials accessible and making patterns discoverable. To help places and things become meaningful in a research context, curate a collection following these steps:

1. **Select:** choose the artifacts you will curate, or identify an existing archive—this can be an old box of stuff, a journal, letters, a drawer of old things, field notes, maps, a digital collection (of pictures, of social media artifacts, of writing, etc.);

2. **Preserve:** take care of your archive—reinforce the box, clean old pictures, back up digital work, label artifacts, and edit the components of your archive;

3. **Present:** collect the work in this archive in a way that will allow you to present it to the class—mount artifacts on a poster, in a book, in a shadow box, etc.; although you've selected a personal archive, make sure not to share parts of the archive that you do not want to be public (within the class);

4. **Analyze:** compose an expository, narrative essay highlighting some of the artifacts in this archive and what they tell us about you at that time and place; and

5. **Reflect:** after you've composed your essay and developed the presentation of your archive, consider how your work might inform future primary research projects that address archives external to your experience.

■ Works Cited

Beauvoir, Simone de. *Letters to Sartre*. Translated and edited by Quintin Hoare, Arcade Publishing, 1993.

Blichfeldt, Malthe Emil, Jonathan Komang-Sønderbek, and Frederik Højlund Westergård. *The Living Tree*. Air Lab, IT University of Copenhagen, 2018. airlab.itu.dk /the-living-tree/.

Dublon, Gershon, and Edwina Portocarrero. *ListenTree. MIT Media Lab,* 2015. listentree.media.mit.edu/.

Sartre, Jean Paul. *Witness to My Life: The Letters of Jean-Paul Sartre to Simone de Beauvoir 1926–1939*. Edited by Simone de Beauvoir, Translated by Lee Fahnestock and Norman MacAfee, Penguin, 1994.

Chapter 7. Working with Visuals

In the spring of 2020, the world was hit with an outbreak of novel coronavirus, the likes of which had not been seen since the Spanish flu of 1918. What were your reactions to the news of this global pandemic? Perhaps you were someone who didn't pay much attention to the news until it reached the United States. Perhaps you had been tracking the outbreak of COVID-19 as it spread country to country. Perhaps you cancelled a vacation or had graduation plans derail. Perhaps you made decisions based on what the news media was showing you. Many political messages at first were quick to try to enforce social distancing—staying home, keeping at least six feet between people when out in public—to try to decrease the chances of infection. Social media was quick to follow, propagating messages of best practices of handwashing and sheltering-in-place. One of the primary things that both kinds of messaging depended on was a particular graphic, shown in Figure 7.1, that showed the spread of the COVID-19 virus with and without the practice of social distancing.

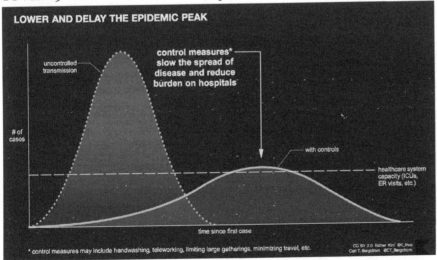

Figure 7.1. Infographic created in 2020 by Esther Kim and Carl T. Bergstrom: Flatten the Curve. Epidemic infographic created for the coronavirus disease 2019 epidemic, but generally applicable for any pandemic.

This visual led both politicians and media professionals around the world to circulate the call to "flatten the curve," referring to the change in shape of the parabola that represented the number of cases of COVID-19 with and without controls like social distancing in place. The hashtag #plankthecurve was used on social media by heads of state to try to encourage these safety measures. After a certain point, the visual itself no longer needed to be used to back up this call, and "flatten the curve" itself became the calling card for engaging in social distancing behavior to slow the pandemic.

This is just one example of the ways that visuals help us think and persuade differently and shows why they are a central method to helping us work with and think through data. Due to an ever-expanding variety of digital technologies for supporting the production of visuals, contemporary scholarly research tends to make greater and greater use of elements such as **photographs**, **graphs**, **tables**, and **data visualizations**. Photographs are realistic images captured with the aid of an instrument (camera) that translates light to a reproducible inscription. Graphs and tables are devices for visually rendering sets of numerical and textual data. And data visualizations is the term used to name other visual readouts or ways of presenting data through visuals, usually with the assistance of a computer.

Generally, as guiding principles, this chapter reinforces the following tenets:

1. **Slow down in the production and reproduction of visuals.***
   Whether finding and selecting visuals made by others or producing your own, the choices we all have include common rhetorical considerations—such as audience and purpose—and design

> What does it mean to slow down in the context of research for you? What areas of your work can afford to move slowly, and at what cost? How might you plan for slowing down parts of your research process?

Try This Together: Visuals that Persuade (30 minutes)

With a partner, come up with a list of five visuals that have been used in recent memory to persuade a public audience to take action. Together, answer the following questions:

- What are the major visual components used (photographs, graphs, tables)?
- What are the major textual components used?
- Where did the visual circulate?
- Why do you think the image circulated as it did?

considerations—such as size, placement, orientation, technical detail, and legibility. Photographers, illustrators, and graphic designers assume careful, reflective stances toward their production processes, and so, too, should you.

2. **Subject visuals to peer review processes much the same as you would with written prose.** The careful, reflective stance noted above often begins by creating a series of drafts and a set of possibilities. A photographer will take several more photos than they will use, then screen the photos, sometimes in consultation with a client, to select photos that depict most effectively the photo's subject. You can achieve the same effect by using a peer review of visuals to measure their effect for an audience.

3. **Develop visuals with attention to accessibility by providing descriptive text and nuanced captions.** Every figure, photograph, illustration, map, table, and graph must include a handle (e.g., Figure 1 or Table 1), a caption (a brief explanation of the visual), and, if you are working in an online environment, descriptive text (a lengthier, more detailed explanation of the visual) that will assure accessibility for assistive readers. We've developed this tenet with greater elaboration further along in this chapter, but we have included it here because it is essential to working with visuals.

4. **Think about the relationship between the visual image and the text.** When working with visuals, writers must decide whether the image is leading the text or the text is leading the image. This question is also known as the imagetext problem for its inquisitive premise: which leads, which follows? If the image is in the lead, its position is likely to be more prominent, perhaps opening the section or appearing at the beginning. If, on the other hand, the image follows, or merely reinforces the text, its position in the document corresponds. It's also possible for image and text to share significance and to work in tandem, each balancing or somehow lending deepened significance to the other. The point here is that when working with visuals, you need to think about the question of a relationship between image and text. Style systems, such as MLA, may require a sequence where the image only appears after it has been men-

tioned in the text. But we regard this as a judgment call that ought to be made in each situation. When image and text are used together, their arrangement and proximity are important to readers engaging with and ultimately understanding how they fit together.

5. **Consult design experts when possible or seek resources on specifications for the best possible display of visuals for print and for screens.** Many experienced artists, designers, and photographers have taken the time to share their wisdom online, preparing and circulating articles and modules on adjusting image size and resolution, positioning the subjects in images for desired effects, working with appropriate file types, and more. We mention this because, when beginning research, many decisions involving visuals you will make have already been made by others, and they can help you. We encourage you to search online for how-to guides, video tutorials, and workarounds for whatever you might encounter.

6. **Give images the same credit-giving citations that apply to textual sources.** When working with images, regard them as the property of the person who created them. Give credit where it is due (see Chapter 2 on ethics), usually in the caption or by-line, but if not, then in a works cited or references entry. Every image you re-use in your own work, whether you found it online or in printed form, must be accompanied by an attribution. While it's true that such attributions require time and attention to detail, they perform an important ethical function, honoring the source of the image and showing regard for the originator.

This chapter introduces working with visuals primarily through the use of photographs, reserving some discussion of graphs, tables, and data visualizations for the end, and concluding with guidance for developing an information graphic.

■ Photographs

With the rise of digital photography over the past two decades, high quality images have become a swift, everyday form of communication. Consider how, from the start of the twentieth century until the rise of digital photography, film cameras required their users to very selectively take photos, carry the film to a development counter or send it to a processor, then wait a couple of days to see whether the photos yielded the desired results. Much scholarly contemplation of the medium of photography took place during the film-based era when development was slower and when photographs were costly and scarce. But contemporary digital photography now makes it possible to swiftly and relatively easily create photographs and incorporate those photographs into written research in mere minutes. This ease raises important questions about the ethics of photo manipulation (touch-ups), cropping, and a growing variety of image-based fakes, though practices of full disclosure head off these concerns for researchers who work with visuals.

Although much has changed for photography, many useful ways of thinking about photography have endured. For example, in his well-known book on photography, *Camera Lucida: Reflections on Photography,* Roland Barthes examined a series of photos that could be grouped generally into two sets: press photos and personal photos. Press photos were those circulating widely on the front pages of major newspapers. Personal photos circulated very differently in that they were oftentimes treated like family heirlooms, privately stored for safekeeping and only occasional viewing. Barthes' distinction between press photos and personal photos is still applicable today as a way to begin thinking about circulation. Many photographs hold value for the person who took them, but they don't bear out the same **rhetorical circulation**,* a phenomenon you might uncover in a visit to the archives. An important point to consider in this context is that just because you value a photograph personally doesn't necessarily mean it will be meaningful in a

Rhetorical circulation names the movement of discourse, taking into consideration materials, timing, and audience uptake. Such circulation is oftentimes mixed and uneven, occurring across digital and physical media, immediately and also with delay, and among intended and unintended audiences.

Try This: Personal and Press Photos (20 minutes)

From a social media platform where you have an account, choose one personal photo you have previously shared. Then choose one press photo used on the website of your city's main newspaper. Consider who has access to each of these photos and how they circulate. What do online spaces offer to our rethinking about the personal value of photos? What has the rise in digital handheld photography meant for re-defining the personal and the press photo?

research context. Writers (revising with input from audiences) establish that significance, usually with direct explanations.

As an analytical framework for describing photos and accounting for their meaning, Barthes introduced a useful vocabulary in his discussions of the terms **studium** and **punctum**. Studium is, generally, what many viewers of a photograph see. It may describe what the photo is generally about. The Big Picture blog from *The Boston Globe* (www3.bostonglobe.com/news /bigpicture) is an excellent resource for noticing studium. Consider, for example, a press photograph of a state fair. The studium, generally, would convey an impression of carnival games, regional agriculture, and festive crowds of people. Punctum, on the other hand, is a highly personal intensity, that which stings or captivates the viewer. Again, in the case of the state fair photograph, punctum is idiosyncratic. It could be the acute noticing of an especially pleasurable (or terrifying) ride, a memory of cotton candy, or a fixation on a mud puddle in the background that someone associates with a childhood visit to a local fairgrounds. In Barthes' influential work on photography, studium and punctum were terms he offered that were helpful for distinguishing between what is generally viewable (shared) in the experience of a photograph and what is only noticed in the visual field (mine alone). We have recalled these terms in part to remind you that terminology used to describe film photography can still be applicable to digital photographs.

Theoretical frameworks like the one Barthes introduced can be helpful as you begin thinking about how photographs connect with research projects. Among your first decisions about photographs will be whether you will be working with your own photographs or using photographs taken by others. Each scenario leads to a related set of questions and considerations:

Try This Together: Studium and Punctum (15 minutes)

Revisit the personal and press photos you chose in the prior activity. How do the concepts of studium and punctum operate in each one? As you talk through your photos with a partner, consider how your discussion helps you think about what is shared and what is singular in the experience of viewing photographs.

If You Are Taking Your Own Photographs*	If You Are Using Photos Taken By Others
• Consider technical features: lighting and positioning, orientation, size and file format, and number of photos. • Will the photos need to be resized for print or for display on a screen (or both)? Will they need to be cropped?	• In addition to considering technical features, make careful note about who took the photograph. • Where did the photograph come from? Is it part of a larger archive? Is it part of a series? Be sure to keep careful records about its context.

A photograph's orientation refers to its longest dimension. If vertical, the long dimension is up and down the page. If horizontal, the long dimension is side to side.

Try This: Working With Selfies (45 minutes)

In precisely what ways are emojis discursive? Discursive means language-like, so, in this sense, the question asks whether emojis are more like words and sentences (units of discourse) or more like images (non-discursive or extra-discursive units).

Choose three facial expression emojis. In only a word or short phrase, label the emotion you associate with the emoji. Next, take a series of selfies in which you try to match the expression of the emoji. Organize the emojis, their labels, and the corresponding photographs into a table. This work can be shared with a partner, a small group, or the entire class. After sharing, consider together some of the following questions:

- What is the relationship among emojis, language, and selfies?
- Are there expressive emotions inadequately conveyed in the current set of emojis?
- Scroll through your most recent text messages. How many emojis do you find in the last ten messages? How many photographs? How many words?
- If emojis are aptly communicative, should they be welcomed into academic discourse? Why or why not?

This final question has potential as a research project. For example, one could develop an interview or survey for students or teachers of writing that asks about attitudes toward emojis. Or, you could take a short piece of writing you've done and introduce emojis into it, then ask readers to describe their experiences reading it. Just by noticing a phenomenon and being curious about it, research questions (and potential projects) begin to take shape.

In certain cases, the subjects of the photos must give permission to be photographed, though this is not the case for what has emerged as a popular type of digital photography, the **selfie**. With a growing body of academic research about selfies and an ever-expanding trove of examples available online, it is increasingly clear that photographing oneself is a popular practice.

■ Cultural Implications of Photography

Research writers who take photos or who use photos must be fully aware of several ethical considerations. This is a significant part of most specialized training in photography, but it is easily overlooked by novices. We have addressed research ethics in more detail in Chapter 2. Here, however, we want to acknowledge that when taking photographs, researchers should always seek **permission**, as it would be a trespass against individual sovereignty to presume approval without asking. In addition to being careful when working with protected groups, as noted in Chapter 2, researchers should remember that cultural values relating to photography vary and must be honored at all times. When someone's worldview (cosmology) differs from your own, you must seek explicit consent before taking photographs of people, sacred sites, ceremonies, or rituals, including all variations of performance (dance, worship) and making (weaving, cooking). When signs are posted that no photography is allowed, these community standards must be respected and followed.

■ Six Specific Types of Photographs Researchers Use

Researchers may use several types of photographs for different reasons, and in this section, we'll expand briefly upon a few. We've associated the types of photographs we discuss and the reasons for using them with example photographs taken along the Lake Michigan shoreline at Ludington State Park in Ludington, Michigan, a place that lends itself to a range of research questions, the most central being, *What are the implications of rising Great Lakes water levels and a resultant disappearing coastline?*

Memory (Recall)

Photographs can help researchers remember details, collect visual samples, and build a record of the context for the samples they collect. For an everyday example, consider the research involved with finding an apartment. Sure, rental companies may provide generic photos online, but taking photos as you look at a series of three or four apartments can help you recall and distinguish their key features. Which one had the purple front door? Which one had an accessibility ramp still being built? These are not usually photos that will be featured in published research, but they nevertheless operate as a potent form of note-keeping. Such photos can also be paired with field notes to help create a more detailed picture of a field site. In addition to being useful for note keeping, photographs can be an aid to invention, helping us notice phenomena in the world that help us generate researchable questions.

For example, consider Figure 7.2, a photograph taken at the edge between the forest and the dunes in Ludington State Park along Michigan's western coastline. The photograph documents a well-trafficked transition point where the wooded overgrowth changes to an open, rolling vista of sandy grasslands. The photograph records this location as data, aiding the recall of a hiker who will want to find the trailhead again on the return hike.

Scene-Establishing (Locative)

As an extension of the field work and site-based observations introduced in Chapter 6, on-location photographs can reveal surrounding factors affecting a great variety of people and issues in the world. A simple photograph of a roadway, for example, can reveal to civil engineers key features of a site study for a prospective project. The same photo can spotlight for an environmental biologist the profile of plants and animals in the immediate vicinity of the road project. It can also pinpoint other seemingly mundane but highly relevant details about signage, sign placement, and visibility. **Scene-establishing photographs** help us list and record what is at a designated location. Paired with other instrument-oriented information, such as soil sample analyses or surface slope measurements, scene-establishing photographs can provide insights into a wide variety of problems, from road hazards to environmental impact.

Figure 7.2. Forest-dune transition at Ludington State Park, Michigan. As the woodlands change over to dunes alongside Lake Michigan, a steep, sandy embankment functions as a trail for hikers to travel. Recording a location like this with a photograph can aid memory. (Image credit: Derek Mueller)

In some fields, scene-establishing photography has taken to the sky and now includes satellite and drone imagery. From these wide scope vantage points, researchers can observe patterns affecting entire regions. Figure 7.3, for example, shows a view of the Lake Michigan coastline facing north from the Big Sable Point Lighthouse in Ludington State Park. The vantage point provides perspective on a changing landscape, as water levels in the Great Lakes have in recent years been rising, resulting in coastal erosion and pooling water inland, both of which impact everything from species habitats to recreation.

Figure 7.3. Lake Michigan's changing coastline. At what rates do the water, sand, and foliated ground shift, and which encroaches on the other over time? This view facing north from atop the Big Sable Point Lighthouse in Ludington State Park in Michigan sets in relationship landform variations where water and land meet. (Image credit: Derek Mueller)

■ Schematic/Technical

In research contexts, **schematic photos** provide plain views useful for assembling complex objects. Schematic photos may help explain the relative sizes of one piece of equipment and another device, or they may, with labeling, provide a guide for quickly reconnecting something like a portable sound system, a desktop telephone, or a computer. Schematic photos are especially common as aids to technical illustration and user documentation for technical and professional writers.

The schematic/technical photo featured in Figure 7.4 (on the next page) includes in it crucial details about a specific product made by Sealite, a marine equipment company, complete with model number and inspector decals. The image shows a highly technical device essential to waterway shipping safety.

■ Artistic/Aesthetic

An artistic or aesthetic use of photographs is usually chosen because they look appealing, because they attract attention to a project, or because they set a mood or elicit a particular feeling, association, or desire. **Artistic/aesthetic* photos** are commonly featured in the slide decks used to present research. For example, a presentation about research on the uptake of ideas, or how ideas catch on and spread, might use as a metaphor for such a process a photograph of a mature dandelion about to be carried off in the wind.

To decide on appropriate artistic/aesthetic photos, consider making a list of concepts or themes that resonate with the research you are doing. These can be metaphors, but you should be careful not to choose metaphors that are overly familiar. Doing so can create an impression that the ideas illuminated by this work rely on tired or long-established commonplaces rather than introducing new and distinctive ways of knowing. The list of concepts or themes you generate provides you with keywords to search for photographs online. Notice how the meaning of Figure 7.5 would change if the image were paired with a tired pun ("Life's a beach") rather than a catchy and inviting tourism catchphrase in a public relations campaign context ("Wander specific") or a more stark and ominous forecast in an environmental sustainability context ("Michigan's vanishing shoreline").

> Artistic/aesthetic photographs can also be selected and incorporated into research publications to focus the audience on a particular association and to impart a lasting impression—whether by interestingness, color scheme, or subject.

Try This: Working with Images and Metaphors (45 minutes)

Returning again to your own research question(s), take or locate a photograph that engages your study metaphorically. What metaphors connect your research to ideas you believe will be engaging to your audience? How clearly and compellingly do you think the photograph elicits these associations? Why?

Figure 7.4. New LED lighting technology in use. Although the Big Sable Point Lighthouse located in Ludington State Park in Ludington, Michigan, was built in 1867 and has illuminated night skies at Michigan's western shoreline for more than a century, the sources of light are smaller today than they once were due to light emitting diodes, or LED lighting. Here, atop the lighthouse, the mismatch of new, smaller technology and older infrastructure is visible only up close; freighters navigating the coastline after dark experience the light's guiding twinkle much as they did before. (Image credit: Derek Mueller)

Figure 7.5. Big Sable Point Lighthouse, Ludington, Michigan. The lighthouse is framed in this case as an attention-getting device, and an aesthetic photograph like this one could be used to express everything from serene themes—such as summertime recreation, beaches, and hiking—to more serious themes—such as historical restoration, the disappearing coastline due to climate change, and the environmental impact of tourism. (Image credit: Derek Mueller)

■ Interaction

Interaction photographs seek to capture moments or events where **interaction** is visible and observable. We welcome you to consider a great range of possible interactions that are relevant for a research project. For example, an interaction photograph could feature two trees, thereby calling into question how they interact, share resources, and connect underground where their root systems and fungal networks make contact. Another example of an interaction photograph could be a picture of a pair of barn swallows, a species of birds noted for their distinctive relationship patterns and habitats. Perhaps most obviously, interaction photographs can also feature humans. In the social sciences, especially, photographic evidence of human interactions sets in sharp relief the intricacies of physical and material surroundings, expressions, and embodiment. Consider Barbara Rogoff's study of children and how they learn by observing and interacting with older children and adults. In the book she wrote about this study, *Apprenticeship in Thinking: Cognitive Development in Social Context,* she included many interaction photographs. This is but one example of many where photographs spotlight interactions and thereby lend insights into the social nature of learning.

Continuing the inquiry into the photographic data available for understanding changes at Ludington State Park, Figure 7.6 spotlights symbiotic interactions at the water's edge and in the precarious zone between the lake itself and the forest.

Figure 7.6. A Monarch butterfly interacting with milkweed plants. Acres of protected greenspace along Lake Michigan's shore in Ludington State Park in Ludington, Michigan, provide habitat that sustains essential interactions between Monarch butterflies and milkweed plants. Milkweed contains a poisonous, milky substance that the Monarch can digest, though this makes the Monarch poisonous to its predators, thereby protecting it from predation. (Image credit: Derek Mueller)

■ Time Series

Photographs have also been used in conducting and presenting research to indicate a **time series**, or changes in a variety of subjects over time. Perhaps the best-known example of this comes from advertising, where before and after photographs of human subjects attest to the validity of some product, usually a diet plan or anti-aging cream. Aside from these commonplace examples, however, researchers have used photographs to study change at intervals. For example, as Marta Braun detailed in her book, *Picturing Time*, French physiologist Étienne-Jules Marey used time series photography to study the phase by phase movements of several subjects, such as a pelican and a human runner. His inquiry into physiological time series also led to early instrumentation now used for measuring heart rate, a development that created a foundation for modern Western medicine. Time series photographs can also illustrate environmental change, showing, for instance, how farms fluctuate over time, how forests manage their shared resources (with and without human involvement), or how rivers change course due to flooding, drought, and irrigation. Photographic evidence can powerfully augment written accounts of a particular question or phenomenon. In the case of Figure 7.7, the photograph is not yet paired with a before or after shot, but as a form of data, it lends time and location-specific evidence of trail flooding in late June at Ludington State Park. How long does this inland flooding last? How many of the last five or ten years has the trail been flooded during the tourism season? A time series photograph would establish data connecting the location to different moments in time, thereby helping us inquire into patterns of interest to park rangers, legislators, tourists, taxpayers, environmental biologists, and more.

■ Positioning, Captioning, and Organizing Images

As a general design principle, unless otherwise designated by a formal style system, such as MLA or APA, or by a set of explicit instructions, you should position images adjacent to the text that makes reference to them. Every figure or image, inclusive of photographs, should be accompanied by a **figure reference**, also known as a handle, and a caption, as we have done throughout this chapter. An example is provided in Figure 7.8. The figure reference, or handle, is a necessary short-form reference that makes it possible to refer to the image from the text. Images lacking a figure reference, or handle, lack an address and therefore can lapse into a faint, inexact relationship with what's written about them.

Figure 7.7. An underwater trail marker. According to park rangers, inland pooling has in recent years become more frequent, creating challenges for maintaining safe and sure hiking trails between the lighthouse and the campground. (Image credit: Derek Mueller)

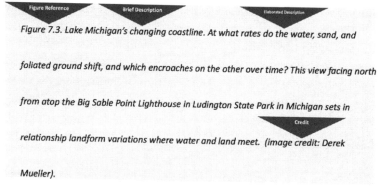

Figure 7.8. Key parts of a caption.

When incorporating more than one image, include sufficient space so that the images and their captions are grouped visually. It should be clear which caption belongs to which image. For reasons of contrast and comparison, it is common for photographs to appear in pairs, especially time series photographs. When presented this way, photographs can prove generative for their striking differences. **Juxtaposition** names the relationship between two photographs intentionally selected for their strongly pronounced differences. The pairing can point sharply to a key concept or theme, commanding attention and setting a lasting impression.

When developing **captions** for photographs you have taken or images you have composed, remember they are authored elements that require careful writing, revision, and proofreading and that they require particular elements that become an essential part of preparing a document that is maximally

---

Try This: What are Other Uses for Photos? (30 minutes)

Research contexts vary greatly, and we recognize there are uses for photography in research beyond the six types we have sketched here. This observation lends itself to a researchable question: How do researchers use photography or photography-related instrumentation (e.g., video, satellite imagery) in an area of study that interests you? How could you learn more about the possibilities or limitations of photography in your area of research interest? Having followed these lines of inquiry, even provisionally, are there any types of photographs you think should be added to the six types we have introduced?

accessible. We've already mentioned that every figure should begin with a figure reference, or handle, such as Figure 1, which is one of these elements needed for accessibility. After the handle, the caption should include a brief description. The language from this description is also appropriate for the image's alternative text when developing online materials, websites, and so on. After the brief description, an additional sentence or two can detail what appears in the image and address the image's purpose. Think of this as an elaborated description and rationale. Finally, depending on the style manual you are following, you might need to include an image credit. With these four elements (**figure reference**, **brief description**, **elaborated description and rationale**, **credit**)* captions will reflect the ethical regard of a researching writer who has honored every reasonable standard for this essential element. All of the captions up to this point include each of these essential elements.

Although we have focused primarily on the use of photographs and their relationship to words in a text, we invite you to consider other multimodal elements that might enhance your composition, such as graphs and tables. Although figures and tables require different in-text citation, similar recommendations for considering the image-text, graph-text, or table-text relationship apply. A final consideration when working with figures, graphs, and tables is organization and **file naming**. Usually original image files are stored separately, outside of the document where you are writing. With this in mind, we recommend creating an online folder for the entire research project where you can store figures and tables in their original format. Research writing with images or tables usually doesn't become too snarled with complexity when there are only one or two visual elements. But because projects like these can

Many contemporary photos online in various places (social media, blogs, some news sites) fail to include all four of these elements in their captions. What do these absences tell you about the ethos of the photographer?

Try This: Understanding Juxtaposition and Captioning (30 minutes)

Using an online image search database, locate two images you find intriguing, compelling, or otherwise generative for reasons you can explain that also reflect a quality of juxtaposition, the condition of inventive spark due to contrastive pairing. Write captions for both images. Then develop a paragraph using appropriate figure references, or handles, to account for how you understand the juxtaposition to be working. What effects, specifically, does this pair of images elicit? Include the vocabulary of "studium" and "punctum" if you find it helpful for discussing the photographs and their significance.

expand to upwards of dozens of images, we recommend exercising care with file naming to stay organized. We encourage you to include basic, consistent information in your file naming as follows: 1) chapter, section, or page number where the visual appears, if applicable; 2) figure or table reference with number; 3) an abbreviated descriptive name; and 4) if you are collaborating with others or working in multiple sections or chapters, some way of identifying yourself with the file.

For example, the file name for the second figure in this chapter would best be presented in the order of chapter, figure reference with number, description, and contributor last name, or 7-fig2-memory-mueller.jpg. If the original file was saved in a special format, it would also be advisable to retain that file as a base version, such as 7-fig2-original.psd. The base version should be off limits to modifications. To make a change, create a copy of the file and adjust the new version. The integrity of the original file can prove vital at later stages of a project's development, such as when publishing.

■ Working with More Visuals

■ Graphs and Tables

Just as with photography, graphs and tables are prone to being underexamined, hastily applied elements even though they are highly specialized elements justifiably associated with quantitative research, statistics, and data analytics. Quantitative research usually undertakes knowledge-making from the standpoint of numbers-driven ways of understanding the world. Quantitative researchers, in other words, use counts of things (measurements, tallies, counts of responses) to express knowledge about phenomena in the world. Therefore, graphs and tables, as common expressions related to quantitative research, also play an important part in qualitative research. Our point in mentioning this is to acknowledge that all researching writers may have cause to introduce graphs or tables for displaying information useful to a research project. You do not need specialized training in statistics or data analytics to incorporate graphs and tables into your research; although, with that said, an introductory course in statistics can help researchers in all fields understand more comprehensively a wide variety of ways of knowing along a complementary, continuous spectrum. It is important to note that though they may portray similar kinds of data, graphs and tables are often handled differently in style manuals. For example, in MLA style, tables are numbered and include a title above the table, while figures, including graphs, are numbered and include a caption below the figure.

Graphs and tables have in common a basic orientation to numerical and arrayed (or list-like) data. Tables, such as the one shown in Table 7.1, show data sets as labeled rows and columns convenient for specific look-ups. Note also how the title precedes the table, while graph titles are located below, as with other figures. Graphs, such as the one in Figure 7.9, organize such data into models that lend themselves to discerning comparisons using basic lines and shapes positioned on a grid. Graphs typically rely upon a strict system of reference (the grid) so they can present with accuracy and consistency positions of values (i.e., addresses) and proportions of geometrical shapes or lines indicative of value. It is quite common for tabular, or table-based, data to also be presented as a graph. Why? The varied forms alter perspective and can thereby heighten attention to meaningful, significant dimensions of the data. Whichever form the data takes, graphs and tables are different possible expressions of data designed with an interest in effective communication. Researching writers who rely upon graphs or tables oftentimes pair these graphical elements with textual accounts in the form of captions and textual passages. This premise is vitally important for researching writers who work with visuals: the image (photograph, graph, table) and text (caption, surrounding discussion)—when developed effectively—are complementary and interdependent. Each needs the other to compel understanding, assent, and action in response to the research.

Extending from the example of the campus tree inventory in Chapter 6, Table 7.1 presents a series of three annual tree censuses from one Midwestern public university. The table shows accurate quantities in rows and columns that aid quick reference. It also raises questions it does not answer. For example, although the adjusted figures (in parentheses) show a net gain, the table does not include details about how many trees were planted or removed.

Table 7.1 Campus Tree Census Table

	2019 Census	2020 Census (Adjusted)	2021 Census (Adjusted)
Deciduous	1479	1790 (+311)	1831 (+41)
Coniferous	3621	4096 (+475)	4211 (+115)
Total survey	**5100**	**5886 (+786)**	**6042 (+156)**

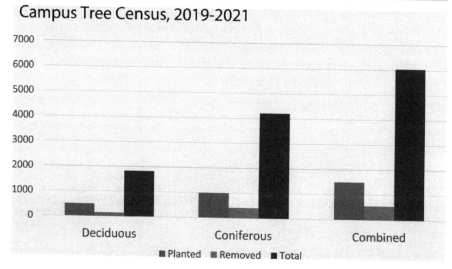

Figure 7.9. A sample bar graph.

It can feel like twice the work to have both image and text operating in tandem, but these echoes and iterations supply readers with depth and dimension that form the basis of research writing.

Tables and graphs often work in tandem with one form, the table, providing granular and specific information, and with the other form, the graph, presenting a visual argument based on a synthesis of the data that may also indicate evidence for trends, clusters, or other patterns. In this case, the tree census data from the table in Table 7.1 is aggregated, or combined, across all three years. The added variable (trees removed) allows viewers to compare how many trees were planted, how many were removed, and where the overall census stands in 2021. A graph like this might be useful for a presentation to a decision maker about the goals for the next three years.

When you choose to work with graphs and tables alongside textual accounts, we recommend seeking a balance between the explanatory power of each. In certain situations, it may be best to adopt with purpose an imbalance, whereby the textual account leads into the graph or table, or, perhaps the opposite is better, whereby the graph or table leads into the textual account.* Whichever the arrangement, you should notice this as a deliberate design, because you, as a researching writer, have command over the sequence.

■ Data Visualizations

Data visualizations is a term used for a large set of graphical forms for displaying data, usually (but not always) with the assistance of computers. Technically, the graphs and tables featured in the previous section are long-established and relatively stable types of data visualizations. Tables visualize data, relying on labeled rows and columns to aid the lookup and cross-referencing of multivariable datasets. Graphs also present data visually, translating numbers into shapes, plots, trend lines, and more. As online tools bloom for presenting data visually, researching writers are presented with a vast number of possibilities for using programs, platforms, and applications to elicit patterns. We urge care and caution when adopting data visualization processes. They can add value, but they can also downplay key details or bury the processes by which they are made. When using a computational process to visualize data, it is the responsibility of

---

Try This: Graphs and Tables (45 minutes)

Locate a contemporary image of data that has been graphed in your local newspaper. Spend 20 minutes reconstructing that data into a table, giving it an appropriate figure reference and caption. In a paragraph, reflect on what, if any, differences you perceive by changing the data's presentation in this way. Is such a change possible when you aren't working with data from your own, original research? Is the data more or less compelling after the change? Do you think the media outlet responsible for the publication considered multiple ways of presenting the data before it decided to publish the version you've worked with?

the researching writer to learn about how the visual is made and to disclose that process before celebrating what can be a spectacular readout.

Think of the growth of data visualization tools today as motivated by the same questions that inspire tables and graphs. What patterns are brought to light by a particular treatment? Why and for whom are these patterns meaningful? In effect, data visualizations should bridge data and the stories you, the researching writer, consider to be at the heart of insights into your research questions. Data visualizations can help writers tell their stories, either deepening patterns or revealing anomalies (breaks from patterns) and their significance. Let us illustrate through three examples ways data visualizations have influenced how we think about specific research questions.

Figure 7.10 is the work of three researchers who collected and coded 154 timely warning crime bulletins circulated at one university over eight years. As required by the Clery Act, also known as the Jeanne Clery Act, all United States

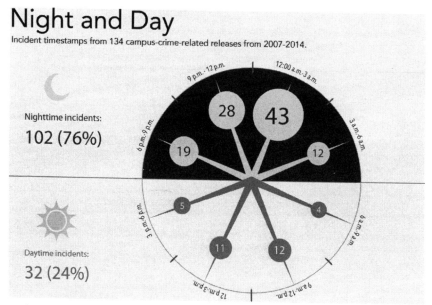

Figure 7.10. Night and Day. A radial diagram displays eight three-hour blocks of time using differently sized circles at the tip of each to indicate the number of crime-reported instances corresponding to each marked off timespan.

colleges and universities must promptly disclose criminal activity in official channels of communication. The research team coded the collection of documents (see Chapter 4 for more on discourse analysis), noting the days and times of the incidents as compared to the days and times of the reports sent out by the university, and as they worked, questions about timing and its effects began to emerge. A vast majority of crime incidents occurred between 9 p.m. and 3 a.m., but the news of these events was distributed during daytime working hours when the university's public relations office opened, resulting in something like an echo effect, whereby the events themselves and the news of the events played around the clock. The research team also coded for the ways the alleged assailants were described in the timely warnings. Here, too, patterns emerged. The patterns were compelling, indicating that 72 percent of the timely warnings attributed criminal activity to a vaguely described assailant whose description was nevertheless associated with race, as shown in Figure 7.11. The full study, these findings, and the discussion of consequences related to these patterns are available online in *Present Tense: A Journal of Rhetoric in Society* (see Pantelides, Mueller, and Green, "Eight Years a 'Wooden Opponent'").

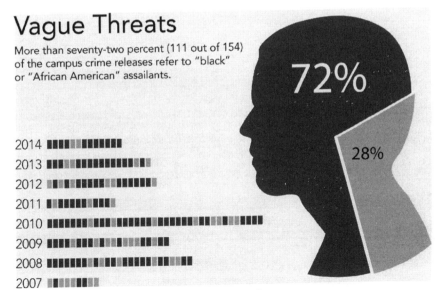

Figure 7.11. Vague Threats.

The data visualization shown in Figure 7.11 reflects prominent sources of data. The first, on the left, introduces a year-by-year count of timely warnings that make reference to an assailant identifiable on the basis of race. The second, on the right, aggregates the year-by-year data, applying it to a human profile color-coded and divided to indicate the disproportionately high rate of timely warnings naming black or African American assailants.

Because Figures 7.10 and 7.11 appeared in a published article, the data visualizations evolved slowly with input from reviewers and editors. Through several drafts and revisions, the versions you see here were made. These visualizations spotlight relationships among quantitative data, emergent patterns, and design choices. In each case, the visualization amplifies data-backed assertions that inform the key conclusions advanced in the full article.

The next example of a **data visualization**,* Figure 7.12, is a census pictograph tied to an inventory of trees on campus. Much like Table 7.1 and Figure 7.9, creating this data visualization helped us develop our research questions. Working with an online report online, students translated the data into a pictograph using two tree type icons in different colors to show the proportion of deciduous trees, coniferous trees, diseased trees, and newly planted trees on campus grounds. Developing a data visualization like this might seem too obvious or boring; however, working

Data visualizations aid researching writers and their readers focus on the most salient, striking insights arising from careful work with data.

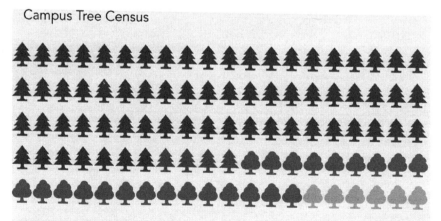

A 2019 tree census established that for every 100 trees on campus, 71 were coniferous and 29 were deciduous. Among the tree population, 4% (all coniferous) were diseased and 6% (all deciduous) had been planted in the last five years.

Figure 7.12. Campus tree census.

with visuals this way adds a striking visual impression to quantitative data. In Figure 7.12, two types of tree icons are color-coded to reflect the percentage of deciduous and coniferous trees on campus, as well as the proportion of diseased trees and newly planted trees corresponding to each major type.

Census pictographs such as Figure 7.12 blend conventional graphing formats, such as bar graphs or pie charts, with **icons** to create a layered visual readout at the juncture between the abstract and the concrete. They communicate neither purely numbers nor purely objects. Instead, in the blended format, quantitative data is brought nearer to the world in which it matters tangibly or in which it applies. This connection between the abstract and the concrete can help us notice important patterns, put a fine point on the implications of research findings, and generate new research questions. Census pictographs can be applied extensively, but they are especially impactful in the context of surveys (see Chapter 5), such as when collecting results from a social media survey, a poll of your classmates, or set of questions you develop that are IRB-approved and that you circulate.

Because time management and accountability for time is a great challenge upon your arrival at college or university, our third and concluding form of data visualization relates to **time use diaries**. An example of this sort of visualization is show in Figure 7.13.

Time	Monday	Tuesday	Wednesday	Thursday	Friday	Saturday	Sunday
8:00 - 8:30 AM		BREAKFAST		BREAKFAST		BREAKFAST	BREAKFAST
8:30 - 9:00 AM				BIOL 130	FR 151 TUTORIAL		
9:00 - 9:30 AM	BREAKFAST	BIOL 130	BREAKFAST			FITNESS	FITNESS
9:30 - 10:00 AM					BREAKFAST		
10:00 - 10:30 AM		READ/STUDY FR 151		READ/STUDY FR 151			
10:30 - 11:00 AM	CHEM 120		CHEM 120		CHEM 120	READ/STUDY BIOL 130	READ/STUDY CHEM 120
11:00 - 11:30 AM		LUNCH		LUNCH			
11:30 - 12:00 PM	FR 151		FR 151		BIOL 130 TUTORIAL		
12:00 - 12:30 PM		HLTH 101		HLTH 101		LUNCH	LUNCH
12:30 - 1:00 PM	PHYS 111		PHYS 111	DAILY REVIEW	PHYS 111		
1:00 - 1:30 PM				PHYS 111		READ/STUDY HLTH 101	READ/STUDY FR 151
1:30 - 2:00 PM	LUNCH	HLTH 101 TUTORIAL	LUNCH	ASSIGNMENT	LUNCH		
2:00 - 2:30 PM	DAILY REVIEW	DAILY REVIEW	DAILY REVIEW				
2:30 - 3:00 PM					PHYS 111 TUTORIAL		
3:00 - 3:30 PM	READ/STUDY BIOL 130	READ/STUDY PHYS 111	READ/STUDY BIOL 130	CHEM 120 LAB	DAILY REVIEW	READ/STUDY PHYS 111	PHYS 111 ASSIGNMENT
3:30 - 4:00 PM	PREP FOR BIOL 130		READ/STUDY FR 151		READ/STUDY CHEM 120		
4:00 - 4:30 PM	LAB						
4:30 - 5:00 PM							
5:00 - 5:30 PM	DINNER	DINNER	DINNER		DINNER	DINNER	DINNER
5:30 - 6:00 PM				DINNER			
6:00 - 6:30 PM		READ/STUDY CHEM 120	READ/STUDY CHEM 120	PHYS 111	READ/STUDY HLTH 101		READ/STUDY BIOL 130
6:30 - 7:00 PM	SCISOC MEETING			ASSIGNMENT			
7:00 - 7:30 PM							PREP FOR TOMORROW
7:30 - 8:00 PM		BIOL 130 LAB		SOCCER INTRAMURALS		SOCIAL/FAMILY	
8:00 - 8:30 PM	FITNESS		FITNESS				
8:30 - 9:00 PM					SOCIAL/FAMILY		
9:00 - 9:30 PM							PLAN FOR THE WEEK
9:30 - 10:00 PM							
10:00 - 10:30 PM	PREP FOR	PREP FOR	PREP FOR	PREP FOR			
10:30 - 11:00 PM	TOMORROW	TOMORROW	TOMORROW	TOMORROW			

Figure 7.13. Time use diary of a science major. Weekly time is divided and color-coded by class subject, meal times, study time, and personal time.

A time use diary enables a bird's-eye view of how a person spends time that does not depend on the same level of detail as found in a daily to-do list (which might include exactly which books you have to read as you study or which food items you ate for breakfast) or a yearly calendar (which might block out special days like holidays, birthdays, or anniversaries). Time use diaries show a snapshot of time and allow you to code and understand, from a middle view, where your time goes.

Try This: Developing a Pictograph (45 minutes)

Plan a draft of a census pictograph based on credible statistical data you locate online. The data could be related to any field or specialization you wish (possibilities include bee ecology and hive health rates, small business startup success rates, publication acceptance rates for journals in your area of study, and much, much more). Hand-draw the pictograph. What design choices, colors, and icons would best suit the data and why? Reflect in a paragraph why you made the choices you did and what might have to change or adapt when revising a hand-drawn image into a digital version.

Try This: Developing a Time Use Diary (60 minutes plus 1 week)

For this activity, begin with a simple spreadsheet or table for recording hours of the day and days of the week. Then, complete the following steps:

1. Develop a system for entering into each cell how you **plan** to spend the time. What labels will you choose, what colors, what symbols, and what will they mean?
2. Using a copy of the same grid, enter into each cell a note or symbol accounting for **how you actually spend time** as the week proceeds. Color-code the cell to indicate simply whether your planning matched with the actual activity.
3. Write vignettes about the system, noting particular hours that were or were not harmonious with your planning.

Over a week, you will have developed an insight into how well-aligned, or felicitous, are your plans and your activities throughout the week.

■ Looking Again at Working with Visuals

In this chapter, we have introduced a few of many possibilities for working with visuals. We have done so in a way that we hope underscores opportunities for research about and with visual rhetorics as well as for the creation of research documents that feature visual elements, such as photographs, graphs, tables, and data visualizations. As you work with visuals and explore those possibilities, we encourage you once more to return to the list of key principles established at the beginning of the chapter:

- Slow down with the production of visuals.
- Subject visuals to peer review processes much the same as applies to the development of written prose.
- Develop visuals with close attention to accessibility by providing descriptive text and detailed captions.
- Think about the relationship between the visual image and the text.
- Consult design experts when possible or seek resources on specifications for the best possible display of visuals for print and for screens.
- Apply the same level of credit-giving citation practices to images that apply to textual sources.

■ Focus on Delivery: The Photo Essay

A photo essay includes a series of photographs that are used to tell a particular story. These essays can be photo-heavy, using only figure references and brief captions to tell a story, or text-heavy, balancing images with paragraphs of explanations. Either way, a photo essay has a narrative arc, or storyline, that informs a reader of a particular message that they should interpret from the images used.

   Using your research question developed throughout Chapter 1, create a photographic essay that brings your research question and some possible leads for inquiry into view. You and your instructor can choose to what degree you want this essay to balance image and text. Some options for blending your research question and images for the photo essay follow:

- Pull a set number of images (with careful attribution) from online databases, and order them in a particular way that lends insight into your researchable question, giving you a few directions or leads to help you move it forward.

- Blend online images with those that you yourself take to reflect your research process or data you've begun collecting.

- Create a photo essay made completely of photographs you take that reflect one or more stages of your research.

- Compose a photo essay featuring photographs of all six types detailed in this chapter that have to do with your research question.

Select just one type of research photograph and then create or find six photographs of that type that shed light on your research topic.

■ Works Cited

Barthes, Roland. *Camera Lucida: Reflections on Photography.* Translated by Richard Howard, Hill and Wang, 1981.

Braun, Marta. *Picturing Time: The Work of Étienne-Jules Marey (1830–1904).* University of Chicago Press, 1995.

"The Jeanne Clery Act." *Clery Center,* clerycenter.org/policy/the-clery-act/.

Pantelides, Kate, Derek N. Mueller, and Gabriel Green. "Eight Years a 'Wooden Opponent': Genre Change (and its Lack) in Campus Timely Warnings." *Present Tense: A Journal of Rhetoric in Society,* vol. 5, no. 1, 2016, www.presenttensejournal.org/volume-5/eight-years-a-wooden-opponent-genre-change-and-its-lack-in-campus-timely-warnings/.

Rogoff, Barbara. *Apprenticeship in Thinking: Cognitive Development in Social Context.* Oxford UP, 1991.

Chapter 8. Research and the Rhetorical Forms It Takes

- Your 5th grade science fair experiment
- A viral video of high school math students rapping the quadratic formula
- A five-minute conversation with a family friend about a summer co-op position at their company based on your community service

These are all ways that research circulates over time, in different locations, through interactions among people and things. This chapter takes into account the ways that research, oftentimes research-in-progress, circulates. **Circulation*** is a contemporary reframing of the rhetorical canon of **delivery**. Delivery, in a classical Greco-Roman rhetorical tradition, was primarily concerned with speakers who, in real-time, stood before reasonably attentive audiences to speak persuasively about matters of civic concern. Over two millennia, as writing systems gained legitimacy and as digital media expanded and flourished, so too did the means of delivery multiply. In today's mediascape, delivery remains relevant, but the mechanisms of delivery have shifted because audiences are themselves producers of recirculation and uptake. That is, someone may read an article and re-post it, watch a video and send it on. Secondary circulation is not a new phenomenon, but it has intensified with the rise of social media and the everyday documentary impulses that proliferate streams of social media. People have their mobile devices out, capturing and relaying the richness and wonder (and also ordinariness and banality) in their surroundings.

To put a finer point on this phenomenon of secondary circulation (i.e., uptake and recirculation), Jim Ridolfo and Dànielle Nicole DeVoss introduced the concept of **rhetorical velocity**. As they explain, rhetorical velocity goes beyond delivery to offer "strategic theorizing for how a text might be recomposed (and why it might be recomposed) by third parties, and how this recom-

Effective research moves into and throughout the world. Delivery and circulation pinpoint how this movement happens.

posing may be useful or not to the short- or long-term rhetorical objectives of the rhetorician." For a researching writer, this means sharing research in such a way that encourages others to do things with it, including to recirculate it. When others take up the work and continue its circulation, rhetorical velocity increases. The reach and influence of the research stands a greater chance of making a difference in the world.

With the goal of setting research in motion, this chapter begins by acknowledging and then challenging two powerful myths connected with research writing. The first myth is that researchers should only share their work with audiences at the end of a research process. The second myth is that beginning researchers should circulate their work only in small circles, to limited audiences, such as the confines of a class and a teacher. Of course, myths emerge from the world around us. These myths in particular about research writing prevail because there are strong cases to be made for circulating research after the study is fully formed and the work completed. Furthermore, circulating research-in-progress to small, supportive, attentive audiences, such as are customarily available in association with a writing class, also makes sense. These myths prevail, in other words, because there are kernels of long-established wisdom etched into them. And yet, we seek here to open these myths with the goal of acknowledging what becomes available when we share about works-in-progress and when we engage audiences broader than the classroom.

Our aim in challenging these myths is to expand perspectives on the potential of rhetorical delivery to clarify and activate research activity as it unfolds. Toward this goal, consider our counter-principles:

Try This Together: Delivery and Circulation (30 minutes)

In a small group, develop definitions of delivery and circulation. How are these terms similar? In what ways do they identify something different? What do you think they mean for researchers who are interested in sharing their work with others?

Discuss how you have participated in rhetorical circulation. That is, have you ever read or viewed something, then passed it along to someone else with the purpose of asking a question, teaching them, deepening their understanding, or changing their mind?

1. **You can, as a writing researcher, share about your work at any moment in the process.** You can write a pre-proposal in which you sketch possible lines of inquiry. You can prepare and deliver a three-minute presentation to your class or your research group at the moment when you are beginning to gather, read, and annotate sources. You can develop for a gallery crawl a draft of a poster that displays decisions you have made about research design, including the questions that interest you most and the potential complications you foresee. With each of these (and many other) possibilities, research is kept social, and the interactions can be generative for you, for your research team if you are collaborating, and for others who are probably working through comparable research processes themselves.

   Delivering the beginning stages of a work-in-progress early and often can help you refine your sense of audience and purpose. The questions you receive will help you make decisions about where to expand, what context to fill in, and what is missing or perhaps understated. It's also possible to revisit a research project long after you believe it was finished and sent off into the world. Five and ten-year retrospectives—look backs—at a research project and asking of it freshly—Why did this work matter? What would I have done differently? How would a comparable study need to be done *now*, were it to be undertaken again?—these and other reflective questions help researchers focus on the longevity of a study's significance, setting it in relationship to time as well as opening new possibilities for continuing or renewed research.

2. **You can, as a writing researcher, share about your work widely, even while it is in-progress or otherwise unfinished, generating and circulating status updates that invite audience engagement.** It may feel risky, yet writing about in-progress research can open your work to outsider feedback, lead to potential collaborations, and build confidence in how you give language to specialized concepts. This is not quite the same as saying you should share everything about the research with other people or that you should post everything about it online. But some measure of practice with delivery and circulation while a project

is underway can help you see it as rhetorical work, connecting it with people who are curious about it. When this happens, research writing can become connected to other stakeholders.

We also want to stress the careful consideration that must go into sharing in-progress work, as this ties in with the discussion of ethics in Chapter 2. Ethical delivery of in-progress research may be focused and invitational, such as by selecting a narrow issue in a study and inviting perspective. It may also proceed with a goal of keeping your work **public facing**, or aimed toward an external audience, and accountable to people who are not researchers but whose lives may be improved by the questions you are asking and what you are learning about those questions. Ethical delivery of in-progress research seeks to emphasize the value of audiences who can participate in the work. We would caution you against disclosures of frustration or complaint about your research process or findings, though missteps, failures, and complications certainly do happen in research and warrant acknowledgement when we are sharing about our work. Finally, a leading goal for wide delivery of in-progress research is to refresh perspective on the classroom as a temporary scene. Research activity often exceeds the length of a semester or quarter.*

> The rhetorical approach to research inquiry we have modeled seeks to keep porous and open the seemingly bounded limits of the writing classroom and the arbitrary time frame of a semester or quarter.

Try This Together: Brainstorming Delivery (15 minutes)

With a partner and using your research topic, question, data collected, or project thus far, generate a list of five to ten ways that you might share in-progress work.

Be sure to consider different kinds of stakeholders—not just your campus community, but your neighborhood, city, hometown, government, workplace, educational, and community groups. Who is affected by your research, and who might want to know a bit more about it? Who would you like to have in an audience that would help you think differently about your research? Then, consider what forms sharing such in-progress work might take. What are some flexible delivery options that an in-progress project might have that a fully finished project does not?

■ The Rhetorical Forms Research Takes

Form usually refers to shape and structure. Certainly there are shapes and structures that have become conventional in interpersonal communication, in workplace communication, in civic and legal communication, and in academic communication. Rhetorical forms, or genres, reflect shapes and structures that have evolved to reflect the values of a particular discourse community. For example, for a legal briefing to be recognizable as a legal briefing, it must assume the shape and structure of legal briefings that have circulated before it. Such a document reflects the unspoken values and expectations of a legal discourse community—the lawyers, judges, and clerks whose communication practices constitute this significant domain of activity. Missing the mark on a particular form risks alienating the discourse community; straying from formal conventions can mean offending important people among the document's audience.

Form becomes rhetorical when it takes into account the communication situation: purpose, audience, context (including forms that have come before it), and timing. This means that form is slightly flexible; rather than adopting a universal, fixed, unchanging view of form, it's better to regard shapes and structures as living, evolving entities. Savvy, effective communicators (rhetors) take this into account each and every time they write. Noticing the evolving qualities of forms, as well as opportunities for new forms that make use of all varieties of media, amounts to **rhetorical awareness**. And it is with rhetorical awareness in mind that we undertake in the remainder of this chapter to introduce general conventions for forms associated with research writing: the IMRAD (an abbreviation for Introduction, Methods, Results, And Discussion) research report, the short form presentation, and the research poster.

■ The IMRAD Research Report

Research reports are the most common form for research delivery and circulation. Although they are written documents primarily constituted by words, they often include graphs, charts, photographs, or figures (see Chapter 7). It is customary for research reports to introduce and contextualize the study, lay out the study's methods and findings, and discuss its consequences, which can include applications, proposed action steps, and prospects for additional research. The scope, or length, of research reports can vary, ranging from abbreviated reports of a few pages, sections, or installments, to larger reports of a few pages, to elaborate accounts of 25 pages or more. What we hope to make clear is that there is no one-size-fits-all research report. Research reports are often similar to one another; however, as rhetorical situations change, often reports do, too. It's important to note conventions are a starting place from which your research writing can adapt to specific situations.

As a general framework for research reports, or what are sometimes called **research papers**, consider the IMRAD research report as one common model. In many STEM-oriented disciplines, the IMRAD report stands out as a basic form. Some have argued it is too basic or too reductive. It is crucial to approach the IMRAD report as an exceedingly basic structure onto which other more nuanced choices should be applied. Many IMRAD research reports will include the four basic sections of introduction, methods, results, and discussion as subheadings, as this can aid readers in finding their way. Here we describe what goes into each of those sections:

- **Introduction:** The opening section of a research report establishes the purpose, or rationale, for the research that follows. It can do this by stating an **opportunity** (or gap in the research), a **problem** the research responds to constructively, or a **question** or series of questions the research answers or deepens. Opportunities, problems, and questions work differently from one field to another, yet they can motivate research in any field. Given this situation, researchers should introduce their work by orienting it to discipline-specific contexts and problems.

- **Methods:** Methods sections account for research design, detailing the choices that go into the ways the researcher has worked. Methods may note timeframes, techniques for recording and coding data, and the methodology—the values backdrop that makes your approach transparent to your audience and to yourself (see Chapter 1). Discussing the **methodology** signals an understanding of disciplinary values, connecting your choices to choices that have been made by others in related research. Coding schemes (Chapter 4) and research memos (Chapter 5) help establish a record of activity that may inform a methods section.

- **Results:** The results section of an IMRAD research report details what happened as the methods were enacted. A results section aligns neatly with laboratory experiments or computational scripts that may be run once, adjusted, and run again. Results, in such cases, can vary. The broader view of results is, in effect, what happened. Results sections account for the activity that followed from the methods presented in the previous section.

- **Discussion:** Discussion is where meaning is opened up and explored. Discussion sections simply and directly attend to questions of consequences by asking, **So what?** This is the section of a report where the research writer interprets the results and makes a case for the results as significant, limited, or altogether failed. Especially when results are limited or failed, there are ample opportunities for renewing questions, refocusing prospective studies, and really learning—establishing **new knowledge** that can be insightful for stakeholders.

Several research report variations stand out in relation to the IMRAD report once this simple shape and structure is established. In some humanities disciplines, texts themselves are the primary form of data. Working with texts—interpreting them, putting them into conversation with one another, and analyzing them for significance—can amount to a research essay. There are also variations of the IMRAD report where interpretation and argumentation take center stage, though the introductory and discussion sections continue to honor the basic functions we've outlined here.

Because research writing is diverse, no single genre can account for the myriad variations you may encounter—whether as a reader or as a writer. There are a few features, however, that distinguish research reports from other genres. Research reports almost always include a references list, or a list of works cited. **References lists** (see Chapter 3, bibliographic phase) provide readers with a comprehensive listing of all sources mentioned in the report. The list makes an ethical gesture—both of giving credit where it is due and of providing readers with a good faith guide they can follow for tracing and finding any source they wish to inquire into more deeply. In some fields, it is also common for research reports to include **footnotes** or **endnotes**—relevant, detailed asides that deepen and contextualize some added dimension of the text. **Appendices** are another common feature of research reports. They are used for including more than the report itself can reasonably incorporate within a specified scope. An appendix is a companion document supplied by the research writer to provide access to a readily available reference, such as reference to a raw data set (e.g., the full script of an interview or supplemental photographs).

■ Short Form Presentations

Much like practice with writing, practice with presentations frequently leads to greater fluency, proficiency, and effectiveness. Presenting helps you hone your own sense of what is appropriate in any given situation and makes you more aware of choices related to timing, the use of media, and audience interaction. Presentations are a rhetorical form for circulating research—whether that research is in its planning stages, well underway, or completed—because they are tailored for a particular audience in a particular place and time.

Try This: Exploring Manuscript Guidelines (45 minutes)

Publishing venues commonly stipulate the forms of research reports they accept. Many predefine a scope, a style system (e.g., MLA, APA, Chicago, etc.), and a stance on the use of footnotes and appendices. Identify one to three publication venues you think might be receptive to publishing research writing like yours. You might start with some of the journals that you came across in your source-work (Chapter 3) or that you have found in your research in the past. Locate the manuscript guidelines for these journals. Which qualities of the document are strictly prescribed? Which appear to you to be less clearly defined? For each publication venue, make a two-column list, with one column identifying strict guidelines and the other identifying features or qualities more loosely determined or not mentioned at all.

Try This, *Too:* Local Publication Venues (30 minutes)

Does your university have a publication venue for the research writing done by undergraduate students? First-year students? Students nearing graduation? Graduate students? Identify these publication venues. How often does this publication come out? What sort of writing is published in it?

Since the early 2000s, short form presentations have caught on in a wide range of fields, from engineering and computer science to rhetoric and design. Short form presentations are sometimes called pitches. Perhaps the best-known type of pitch is the **elevator pitch,*** named for its duration approximating the time it takes to tell someone on an elevator about something you are doing, selling, or working on. Even the longest elevator ride is only a few minutes. Elevator pitches, then, are purposefully bound at only a few minutes. Presenters delivering elevator pitches have a short timeframe to get to the point, deliver a key premise or two, or pose a couple of questions, perhaps; ultimately, they must keep it short and sweet.

Several other short form presentations have gained notoriety in recent years. The **PechaKucha** presentation, a model devised by engineers who were impatient with needlessly drawn out presentations, is usually made up of 20 slides, each set to automatically rotate after 20 seconds. This makes for a 6 minute, 40 second presentation. **Ignite presentations** work similarly; these are five minute presentations with automatically advancing slides. Twenty slides advance after 15 seconds each, making for a five minute pitch. And the **Three Minute Thesis** presentation, popularized first at Queensland University in Australia, comes in at strictly three minutes using one slide.

Whatever the specifications for a short form presentation, we urge an awareness of the rhetorical considerations consistent with other forms of communication—audience, purpose, timing, and context. Effective short form presentations focus only on one or two major ideas; they are spare in that they are long enough to offer only a provocation or provide only a slice of a research study, which then stages the possibility of more expansive discussion.

We want to highlight a few additional considerations as you undertake a short form presentation yourself in order to highlight the idea that research can be shared or circulated at *any moment in its development:*

1. **Slide decks for digitally-enhanced presentations are composed.** They are written, assembled, arranged, and configured with regard to specific audiences and purposes. Because slide decks are written, they should be developed with rhetorical consideration and care that reflects the choices of the presenter and an awareness of audience. This means paying close attention to the number of words, to the spare and

> When preparing and delivering an elevator pitch, or a short form presentation, rhetorical considerations of audience, purpose, timing, and context are paramount.

purposeful use of images that give appropriate credit to sources, and to the choices that go into typeface, spacing, and color coordination. None of these features should be shrugged off as unimportant, for the slide deck carries with it the ethos of the presenter.

2. **The presentation itself is only a part of the purpose.** It's true that the presenter delivers information, sharing details about the research process and findings, but the presenter is also responsible for setting the tone for the kind of conversation they want to have after the presentation. Presenters should encourage questions and answers, perhaps by including a slide at the end that invites questions, whether general or specific.

Try This: What Makes an Effective Short Form Presentation? (30 minutes)

Look into the short form presentations listed here: PechaKucha, Ignite, and Three Minute Thesis (3MT). See if you can find online one presentation adhering to one of these formats that you consider to be effective for any of the following reasons:

- the clarity of its main point or central idea
- its use of typeface and spacing
- its use of color and images
- the relationship between the language of the speaker and the language on the slides
- the question or questions posed in the presentation

Identify one of these qualities and describe why you think the presentation is rhetorically effective on this basis.

Try This, Too: Presenting Visuals (45 minutes)

As you consider possibilities for focusing and developing your own short form presentation, return to Chapter 7: Working with Visuals. Which visuals do you think would align well with your presentation? Why? Identify up to three visuals and write rationale statements for why they would make a worthwhile addition to the short form presentation you are developing. If you choose photographs, what are some advantages in taking or choosing to work with your own photographs rather than locating and incorporating images you find online?

3. **Short form presentations can be integrated and coordinated for what are sometimes called group presentations.** When teams of researchers collaborate on a research project, group presentations can be an opportunity for them to share information about their roles and the intricacies of their work insofar as they shaped the study and conducted dimensions of the research. Short form presentations also work well for coordinated panels and roundtables, leaving sufficient time in classes or conferences featuring such presentations for conversation and discussion.

■ Research Posters

Research posters are yet another common rhetorical form used for delivering and circulating research. Research posters can put on display central claims and assertions, questions or lines of inquiry, and provisional findings and snapshots or slices of data. They might pick and choose among data presented in words or presented visually, such as in graphs, charts, tables, and infographics (see Chapter 7). They may even re-format IMRAD report findings visually. Posters reflect design choices that impact typeface and size, spacing and positioning, figures and captions, and references.

In some disciplines, posters reflect a widely shared grammar, or pattern. This means that a sample of posters will reflect similar features. In other disciplines, however, design choices reflect greater variety, and, as such, no two posters adhere to the same formula. Research posters can be designed for a great range of shapes and sizes, from minimalist formats, like 11x17-inch flyers, which don't allow for much content, to 48x36-inch posters, which can feature greater numbers of images and higher word counts. It is hard to generalize about all posters. Some research posters, for example, have been remediated for digital environments, which means there are so-called digital posters in circulation that blur distinctions between large PDF documents, web sites, and slide decks.

Many posters are put on display during what are called **poster sessions**, or scheduled events during which presenters stand or sit nearby the poster while attendees browse as if making their way through a gallery. One advantage of this model is that the researcher who created the poster is nearby for talking conversationally about the research. But this real-time interaction also means that posters should be designed thoughtfully with regard to legibility (large text and understandable images). Posters browsed in a gallery setting should also be direct about questions or provocations, even highlighting the takeaway for those who are interested in learning about the study, its status, and its prospective insights.

■ Expanding Forms

In addition to research reports, short form presentations, and research posters, many other rhetorical forms have extended the reach and circulation of research beyond classrooms and campuses. Some universities host research fairs where researchers share their work using mixed forms—websites, podcasts, dioramas, brochures, pamphlets, short documentary videos, handouts, games, and zines. Working across these rhetorical forms is called **multimodal transformation**, for it recognizes and takes seriously (and sometimes playfully, too) the principles that research should circulate widely and also that the widest possible circulation benefits from recompositions between one form and another. Making good use of a wide array of choices for presenting research, both in-process and finished, can help researchers discover new audiences and connect with prospective stakeholders and can also generate **rhetorical velocity** for researchers as others reformulate their findings as well.

▌ Focus on Delivery: Developing a Research Poster

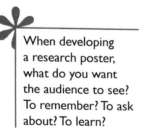

When developing a research poster, what do you want the audience to see? To remember? To ask about? To learn?

Research posters* involve considerations of timing, audience, and purpose. How much time do you have to develop the poster and for how long will it be on display? Who is likely to see the poster, to ask questions about it, to engage with it while you, as its maker, are or are not present? What goals do you have for the poster? Do you want it to provide an update, to pose questions, to share results and analysis, or to pose possibilities for future, related research? These generative lead-ins should help you begin to sketch out a plan for the poster, which can then shift to secondary considerations that are more practical and applied, related to size and materials.

In terms of sizes and materials, a crucial consideration from the outset is whether you will design the poster to be printed as an entire work or whether, instead, you will work with smaller pieces (e.g., standard sheets of paper cut and pasted or taped into place). For printed posters, PowerPoint, Google Slides, or other slideware can provide you with a canvas, which you can size to the desired specifications and output as a PDF. When working with one of these programs, we recommend beginning with a white background and black text, as these defaults match best with standard paper colors and high contrast printing results.

Before you commit to creating a poster digitally to later save it as a PDF for printing, look into printing options on your campus or nearby. What printing options are there? What will it cost to print the poster? What else will you need to have on hand to assure that it stands upright during the poster presentation? Will you need tape or tacks? Will there be an easel? These seemingly rudimentary details about displaying a research poster are the responsibility of the presenter putting it on display. Neglecting to attend to these important, practical details can lead to surprising costs, or, even worse, the unfortunate situation of not being able to display your poster on the day of the session.

Standard poster boards are 22x28 inches or 24x36 inches, while medium display tri-folds are 36x48 inches. Because these sizes are variable, the first time you create a poster, it may be best to work with smaller elements that you attach to the board. This strategy gives you options for focusing on specific elements if you decide you need to make an adjustment once you display the poster.

At a minimum, a research poster should include

- a prominent title
- the researcher's name and contact information (email address, at a minimum)
- a handout or a link to references

Other options for content on a research poster include

- a statement about the purpose for the research, including the design of the study and provisional findings
- up to two specific assertions, insights, or discoveries realized through analysis

- up to two specific limitations, constraints, or shortcomings encountered while undertaking the study

- up to two questions or prospective possibilities for further research, including next steps

- at least one visual element, such as a photograph, graph or chart, table, or infographic (see Chapter 7)

As you develop your poster, remember that those who read it will almost always be viewing it from a distance of three to five feet, so larger typefaces (e.g., 24 point) and high contrast color choices (e.g., no yellows, pinks, or light blues) will give your poster the best chance of communicating effectively to the audience.

■ Works Cited

Ridolfo, Jim, and Dànielle Nicole DeVoss. "Composing for Recomposition: Rhetorical Velocity and Delivery." *Kairos: A Journal of Rhetoric, Technology, and Pedagogy,* vol. 13, no. 2, 2009, kairos.technorhetoric.net/13.2/topoi/ridolfo_devoss/index.html.

Try This: Creating a Research Methods Glossary (1 hour or more)

Throughout this book, we have boldfaced several keywords and phrases we consider significant for gaining practice with research methods. In some cases, the boldfaced words are accompanied by an in-text definition. In other cases, the keyword or phrase is boldfaced but the definition is implied within a section or chapter's broader context. And in yet other cases, the term may warrant more careful searching—defining keywords as an act of research. Rather than provide a fixed glossary, we offer this final Try This as an invitation to develop your own research methods glossary. You might build the glossary and compile its definitions working only with the boldfaced terms, or you might explore beyond the bounds of this book to introduce other relevant vocabulary. You might build the glossary individually, as part of a working group, or as a class. And you might build the glossary quickly or over many weeks or months, returning to established terms and definitions to fine tune them based on your experience with research writing and informed by all you are learning. We invite you to try this, in this way, because we consider writing a glossary to be an act of composing that is generative and that is well matched with the most rewarding possible engagements with research writing.

Acknowledgments

- Figure 3.6. Alonda Johnson.

- Figure 3.7. 3D worknet model by Alonda Johnson.

- Figure 7.1. Image created by Esther Kim (@k_thos) and Carl T. Bergstrom (@CT_Bergstrom). Obtained through Wikimedia at https://commons.wikimedia.org/wiki/File:Flatten_the_curve_-_coronavirus_disease_2019_epidemic_infographic.jpg. Used under a Creative Commons Attribution 2.0 Generic license.

- Figure 7.10. This figure was previously published in Kate Pantelides, Derek N. Mueller, and Gabriel Green, "Eight Years a 'Wooden Opponent': Genre Change (and its Lack) in Campus Timely Warnings." Present Tense: A Journal of Rhetoric in Society, vol. 5, no. 1, 2016, www.presenttensejournal.org/volume-5/eight-years-a-wooden-opponent-genre-change-and-its-lack-in-campus-timely-warnings/ and is reprinted under the Creative Commons Attribution-Noncommercial-Share Alike 3.0 United States License.

- Figure 7.11. This figure was previously published in Kate Pantelides, Derek N. Mueller, and Gabriel Green, "Eight Years a 'Wooden Opponent': Genre Change (and its Lack) in Campus Timely Warnings." *Present Tense: A Journal of Rhetoric in Society, vol. 5, no. 1, 2016,* www.presenttensejournal.org/volume-5/eight-years-a-wooden-opponent-genre-change-and-its-lack-in-campus-timely-warnings/ and is reprinted under the Creative Commons Attribution-Noncommercial-Share Alike 3.0 United States License.